7.0), Combined 20.5 (13.8) – 37.7 (7.5). CO2 emissions g/km: 322 - 196.

# LAND ROVER CON

## 7
### DESIGN

## 39
### THE JOURNEY

## 83
### INNOVATION

**EDITOR-IN-CHIEF** Steve Fowler

**EDITOR** Dan Stevens

**CREATIVE DIRECTOR** Ash Gibson

**ART DIRECTOR** Kerem Shefik

**PRODUCTION EDITOR** Matthew Rigby

**SUB EDITORS** Stephen Errity, Sarah Wakely

**CONTRIBUTORS** Mike Duff, Tom Phillips, Jack Rix, Alistair Weaver, Matt Howell, Otis Clay

**THANKS TO** Land Rover's Lindsey Dipple, Aimee Hancock, Jamie McGeachy, Rachel Murray, Kim Palmer and Lucy Reynolds

**PHOTOGRAPHY**

British Pathé (p021), Alamy (p030), Stahl House (p031), Nick Dimbleby (p056, 061), Matt Howell (p074), Matt Vosper (p104)

**LICENSING & SYNDICATION**

To license this product please contact Carlotta Serantoni on +44 (0) 20 79076550 or email carlotta_serantoni@dennis.co.uk To syndicate content from this product please contact Anj Dosaj Halai on +44(0) 20 7907 6132 or email anj_dosaj-halai@dennis.co.uk

**MANAGEMENT**

**MAGBOOK PUBLISHER**
Dharmesh Mistry

**OPERATIONS DIRECTOR** Robin Ryan

**MD OF ADVERTISING**
Julian Lloyd-Evans

**NEWSTRADE DIRECTOR** David Barker

**MD OF ENTERPRISE** Martin Belson

**CHIEF OPERATING OFFICER**
Brett Reynolds

**GROUP FINANCE DIRECTOR** Ian Leggett

**CHIEF EXECUTIVE** James Tye

**CHAIRMAN** Felix Dennis

# NTENTS

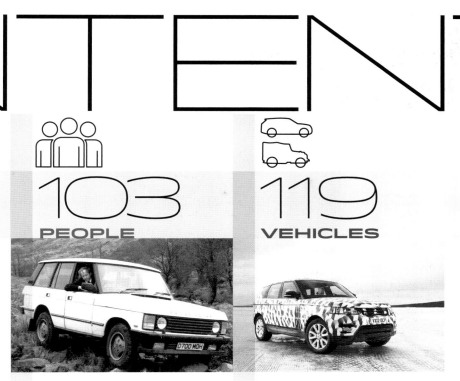

**MAGBOOK**

The MagBook brand is a trademark of Dennis Publishing Ltd. 30 Cleveland St, London W1T 4JD. Company registered in England. All material © Dennis Publishing Ltd, licensed by Felden 2013, and may not be reproduced in whole or part without the consent of the publishers. Land Rover - Past, Present and Future
ISBN 1-78106-208-0

### LIABILITY

While every care was taken during the production of this MagBook, the publishers cannot be held responsible for the accuracy of the information or any consequence arising from it. Dennis Publishing takes no responsibility for the companies advertising in this MagBook. The paper used within this MagBook is produced from sustainable fibre, manufactured by mills with a valid chain of custody. Printed at Polestar Bicester

AS LAND ROVER celebrates its 65th birthday, the company couldn't be in better shape. An all-new Range Rover family has been launched within the space of three years, a refreshed Freelander has gone on sale, the Discovery is still one of the finest 4x4s on the planet and the Defender is cementing its iconic status with each passing year, the future is looking stronger than ever.

To celebrate the great achievements of this great British brand, we at Auto Express wanted to look back at what has helped to get Land Rover where it is today, and look forward to its even bright future.

That's why we've created this collector's Magbook – it's for anyone with a love of Land Rovers, whether that's as an existing owner, a potential owner or someone who has one parked on their dream driveway.

We've had exclusive access to the latest model, the Range Rover Sport, and to the people behind the current award-winning range of cars. We've tested Land Rovers in the extreme conditions they were built for and taken things slightly more sedately in some of the historic cars that the brand is so proud of.

Every model is covered in great detail, with lavish photography – there's even a timeline of every Land Rover to be launched over the past 65 years.

So what does the future hold? We know the range will expand further still, while replacements for existing favourites are in the pipeline, too.

It's an exciting time for Land Rover and an exciting time for us to be covering its great products. We hope you enjoy this celebration as much as we did putting it together.

**Steve Fowler**
**Editor-in-chief**

## We've tested Land Rovers in the extreme conditions they were built for

# LAND ROVER

# THE DESIGN

**Where it all starts and where it all started, from the very new Range Rover Sport to the genesis of the Land Rover 65 years ago**

# RANGE ROVER SPORT
## THE FULL STORY

The team behind the all-new Range Rover Sport gives us a guided tour of the brand's newest model

# W

**WITHIN THE SPACE** of two years, the new Range Rover family is complete. First came the Evoque, swiftly followed by the Range Rover, and now the new Range Rover Sport is heading for showrooms. On its own, the Sport is a striking machine: mixing styling cues from other models with a new level of dynamics and agility into a super-luxurious sports utility vehicle. With the Sport stood between its siblings, the journey from smallest to largest is clear. Land Rover's design director, Gerry McGovern, and his team have done an outstanding job creating a harmonious family look.

The new Sport sits on the same lightweight platform as the latest Range Rover, but 75 per cent of the car is unique. It has an all-aluminium body, which shaves 500kg off the weight of the equivalent previous model. That car was launched back in 2005 as the second member of the product family. Although it shared styling cues with the Range Rover of the time, it was actually based on the contemporary Land Rover Discovery.

"The old model was quite conservative in its design," explains McGovern. "With the new Sport, we wanted to pull it away from the Range Rover to give it its own personality." The company DNA is clear: a clamshell bonnet, floating roof and continuous waistline. Then there are the unique Sport features, such as the bumper vents and the lower shape.

The new Sport has a lower centre of gravity and what McGovern describes as "killer proportions". Viewed directly from the front or rear, it looks surprisingly squat and muscular, while from the side it looks long, sleek and fast as the roofline drops down towards the back to meet the rising waistline. "The Evoque has a more 'cabin forward' style, which we've managed to achieve thanks to the transversely mounted engines," says McGovern. "With the Range Rover Sport, the tension moves towards the back of the car. There's a similar commanding driving position to the Evoque, whereas the Range Rover is more upright and stately – presidential, even."

The Sport is clearly less formal than the Range Rover – you could even call it relaxed – and while the Range Rover gets a deep grille with three bars, the Sport's is shallower, with just two bars. There's more verticality to the Range Rover, with deeper side glass. "The new model has a higher beltline than the outgoing car," says McGovern, "That looked a little bit like a viewing gallery on wheels." According to Land Rover, women drivers feel safer in a car with a higher beltline, and the Sport is likely to have a greater proportion of female drivers than the Range Rover.

McGovern describes an imaginary line that can be drawn through the A-pillars and directly down through the centre of the front wheel – another Range Rover feature that gives the car a "paw-like" stance. The slim headlights and tail-lamps are not unlike the larger car's, wrapping around the bodywork. "They're accentuated more than on the Range Rover," he explains, and

**TOP**
Sweeping design of the new Sport's headlights is one of several visual touches inspired by the Evoque

**MIDDLE**
Sport's grille has two bars and is less upright than the Range Rover's, emphasising its dynamic nature

**ABOVE**
Xenon headlights on the new Sport feature a detailed design that incorporates the Range Rover logo

"The new Sport mixes styling cues from the smaller Evoque and larger Range Rover into a purposeful, poised and luxurious sports utility vehicle"

**ABOVE + LEFT**
Land Rover's designers had a clear brief to make the new Sport as dynamically accomplished as possible, while still retaining the brand's famed off-road credentials. Lightweight chassis and hi-tech Terrain Response System ensure both aims are achieved

**BELOW**
Sport gets a third row of seats for the first time. They sit hidden in the boot floor and will rise at the touch of a button whenever they're required

**RIGHT**
Driving position is lower, with a more cocooned feeling that's reminiscent of Evoque rather than Range Rover. Gear selector is a stick and paddles rather than Range Rover's rotary selector

"The interior is a blend of dynamism and luxury, which is something Land Rover knows a thing or two about"

they're in line with the central axis, which reduces the length of the car and makes it look tighter and more resolved." And although the vents on the front bumpers and bonnet are purely cosmetic, McGovern is quick to stress that "every line has a reason".

Nick Rogers is Vehicle Line Director for the Range Rover models, with responsibility for developing the cars and putting them into production. He describes some of the processes the new Sport went through. "The 2010 Range Rover Sport was an important step for us – it moved the car further upmarket. With the new Range Rover, we had a blank sheet of paper, and that model has the legs to become even more premium. And with this Sport, we had two blank sheets – no expense was spared to make this the most dynamic Range Rover to drive that we've ever built."

Overall, the Sport looks smaller than the Range Rover, but its wheelbase is near-enough identical, which helps give it a lower, sportier stance. The wheelbase is a sizeable 178mm longer than the old car, while the track is wider, too.

Much of the advanced chassis technology from the new Range Rover is also found on the Sport, but it's been adjusted for greater dynamism. "The Sport gets Active Roll Control and the actuator is basically the same as in the Range Rover," explains Rogers, "but the attachment point is different, which allows greater leverage." Combined with the 500kg weight saving, that should ensure the Sport corners with less body roll and greater grip.

"Land Rover is now the world leader in aluminium vehicle body technology," says Rogers. "We have the world's largest aluminium bodyshop and a second one of the same size is about to be built. Every rivet is applied by robots, which is the key to manufacturing accuracy and the durability of the completed body shell."

While much is made of the new model's sporting prowess, it still wears a Land Rover badge, so it needs to demonstrate off-road ability, too. "We've made it much better off-road, with more wheel travel than before – up to 580mm compared with 420mm for a BMW X5," says Rogers. "It has the latest Terrain Response System, too, which reacts automatically to changes in surfaces and terrain up to 500 times a second." As well as presets for different types of off-roading, there's also a dynamic mode for a sportier drive.

The new Range Rover Sport will be available with the widest-ever range of engines, most of which will be shared with the

**LEFT**
Sport's in-car entertainment system includes neatly integrated screens set into the back of the front headrests

**LEFT, ABOVE**
Dashboard has 50 per cent fewer switches than before, with many controls now on a touchscreen or at the driver's fingertips on the steering wheel

**ABOVE**
According to Land Rover, the higher beltline should appeal to women, who like the feeling of safety it brings. More women are likely to buy Sports than Range Rovers

"While much is made of the new model's sporting prowess, it still wears a Land Rover badge, so it needs to demonstrate great off-road ability, too"

At launch, the Sport will be available with a V6 diesel engine and the range-topping 5.0-litre supercharged petrol V8. A V8 diesel and a lower-powered V6 will come later

**LEFT**
Dynamic mode improves the responsiveness of the Sport's throttle, brakes and steering for sharper handling

**RIGHT**
New Sport has a wheelbase that's 178mm longer than the old model's, making the car look lower, sleeker and sportier than it did before

"Although the Sport costs less than a Range Rover, there's no difference in interior quality"

**LEFT**
Whereas the new Range Rover is intended to be the last word in luxury, the Sport aims to involve its occupants more closely in the driving experience

Range Rover. These include V6 and V8 diesels, plus the 5.0-litre supercharged V8 petrol. Jaguar Land Rover's new 3.0-litre V6 petrol will also be available, while four-cylinder engines, as well as hybrid powertrains will eventually appear.

The interior perfectly blends dynamism and luxury – something Land Rover knows a thing or two about. "Our senior managers go on a course that immerses them in luxury," explains Gerry McGovern. "They visit Saville Row tailors to get an idea of who our customers are and what levels of luxury they might experience."

Although the Sport costs less than a Range Rover, there's no difference in interior quality. You'll notice a more angled fascia and higher central tunnel in the Sport, which enhance the feeling of sportiness. With a higher waistline than the Range Rover, the Sport feels snugger inside – something else that appeals to female buyers.

One big change for the new model that stirred much debate within the company was replacing the rotary gearbox controller (the one that rises majestically when the car starts) with a stick and steering wheel paddles. The Sport's wheel is smaller than the Range Rover's, and it has sportier graphics on its twin-pod instrument binnacle. However, the top-spec Autobiography model has a Range Rover-style TFT display.

A touchscreen controls the infotainment system, and Rogers says there are 50 per cent fewer dash switches than in the old car. Many have been moved into the screen, which has fast keys on either side for shortcuts. A full-length panoramic roof will also be available, having proved a huge hit with customers of other models. As in the Range Rover, Meridian provides the entertainment system, which bodes well for audiophiles. And further technology enhancements to come include a head-up display and remote control of the heating and sat-nav systems.

The combination of a slightly longer wheelbase and slightly lower ride height makes it easier to get into the back of the Sport than the Range Rover. And once you're in, there's plenty of knee and headroom. This will also be the first-ever Range Rover with an optional seven-seater configuration. Hidden under the boot floor are two leather seats, which rise into position at the press of a button. According to Rogers, they've been designed for an average European 14-year-old, making the car more of a 5+2.

In true Range Rover style, the Sport was launched at a stunning, star-spangled party ahead of the New York Motor Show. The location was chosen because the city has more Range Rover Sport owners than anywhere else in the world.

With the US market growing fast, and strong sales being recorded across Europe, the Middle East and especially China, this new Range Rover Sport looks to have the perfect blend of talents to play a significant part in continuing the brand's successful march forwards for another 65 years. LR

# STRANGE ROVERS

The Land Rover was designed to work, and the adaptable nature of its design made it perfect for all sorts of unusual conversions, from turning it into a hovercraft to grafting on the back end of a tank

## BIGFOOT 2007
### Land Rover Specialist Vehicles

**OFFICIALLY, BIGFOOT** was built to act as a support vehicle on Land Rover launches, which tend to happen in places with challenging terrain, such as Finland and Morocco. But the mini-monster-truck Defenders – there are two of them – became something of an attraction in their own right, helped by the fact that they were built by Land Rover Special Vehicles; which in essence means that they were done properly.

Inside, they have a device called an underdrive: essentially an ultra-low-range gearbox that allows the vehicle to move incredibly slowly over very difficult terrain, such as unforgiving rocks. The underdrive's fifth gear is equivalent to a Defender's low-range first, which makes the Bigfoot extremely controllable. It also means that the vehicle can tackle incredibly steep hills, even with loose surfaces, which tend to halt progress.

Add locking differentials and a whopping-great set of 38-inch tyres that can be deflated to just 3psi for dealing with soft ground, and you've created one of the most capable Defenders ever built.

**BELOW**
This pair of Land Rover launch support vehicles employ an ultra low-range gearbox, which allows them to crawl extremely slowly over awkward terrain. They ride on enormous tyres; if the driver finds himself on soft snow or sand, they can be deflated to 3psi to vastly improve grip

**RIGHT AND BELOW**
The triangular caterpillar tracks fitted to the Cuthbertson look ungainly, but they allowed it to tip-toe across soft ground. But steep slopes were best avoided

CUTHBERTSON 1963
Cuthbertson

**OBVIOUSLY THE** best way of making a Land Rover utterly unstoppable off-road is to turn it into a tank. Okay, so this one didn't get a gun, but the Cuthbertson conversion did receive four sets of caterpillar tracks, each driven by the Land Rover's wheels. It looks complex and even a bit awkward, perched on top of its triangular track sets, but it was pretty simple and very capable – provided you didn't need to cross any steep slopes at an angle (when it tended to tumble over). A chainwheel bolted to the axle hubs propelled the tracks, and the front pair turned to steer the vehicle. That was it.

The advantage of tracks is that they allow a vehicle to cross really soft ground, because they spread the load more evenly than a set of tyres. Military bomb-disposal squads liked the Cuthbertson, as it could reach all sorts of inaccessible locations.

As a tool, the Cuthbertson design was a success, carrying on into the early eighties. The triangular track concept was also revived by Land Rover on a couple of 110s built for a factory-run expedition.

FOREST ROVER 1961
Roadless Traction

**LEFT**
The Forest Rover had ground clearance of 432mm, which helped it drive over fallen trees. Underneath the modified bodywork lurked a standard Land Rover, though, including the 2.25-litre engine and regular brakes. A 40-foot turning circle certainly worked against it on the road

**BELOW**
The first amphibious Land Rover (bottom) had airbag-style flotation devices, but these made the car vulnerable as a military vehicle. The second prototype moved its flotation tanks inboard

AMPHIBIOUS 1963↓ & 1965↑
Land Rover

**ESSENTIALLY THIS** is a short-wheelbase Land Rover with a set of 28-inch tractor tyres attached to new axles, and some radically chopped-about bodywork to accommodate those tyres. There's a bit more to the Forest Rover, though: it was created to tackle logging tracks and traverse fallen trees, in the same way that a forestry tractor could. The mighty tyres increased ground clearance to an impressive 432mm, and gave the vehicle the ability to drive through the kind of ruts that would swallow a standard Land Rover whole.

Astonishingly, given the enormous wheels and tyres, and the strain that they must have inflicted on the drivetrain, the rest of the Forest Rover was standard Land Rover: gearbox, engine (all 2286cc of it), propshafts, steering and even the brakes. Okay, so it was incredibly slow (30mph flat-out), and had a 40ft turning circle which made it very hard work on the road; but the clearance and tyre size enabled it to do its job, and do it well.

It's exceptionally rare now – only about 20 were made, and most of those ended up abroad.

**THAT AUTOMOTIVE** dream of the 1960s – a car that was also a boat – was realised in a couple of quite serious vehicles for the military, although the amphibious Land Rover idea never made it beyond the experimental stage.

The design of the first example included the attachment of inflatable bags to the side of a Land Rover to make it float. A prop attached to the rear diff powered it in the water, although oddly it was faster going backwards than forwards. The vehicle wasn't put into service, as it took ages to fit the bags; it would also have been easy for the whole concept to be literally scuppered by a single shot to the bags. The idea of fitting outside airbags to a Land Rover has been used by the company more recently on promotional vehicles, such as the Discovery built for Cowes Week in 1990.

The second attempt was designed for the Australian Army, and incorporated the flotation devices into the bodywork (which was hollow and filled with foam); this made the whole thing look much more purposeful. It didn't need hours of setting up, and wouldn't sink if hit by a bullet. But, like its predecessor, it wasn't commissioned for production.

## HOVER ROVER 1962
**Vickers Armstrong**

## CENTAUR 1978
**Laird**

**THE MOST** complicated and expensive conversion ever carried out on a Land Rover turned it into a hovercraft. It never actually needed to be one, but Vickers had just started building hovercraft, and decided that the Land Rover would really benefit from being able to float across rough terrain.

The result was a huge skirt surrounding the vehicle, with a pair of fans fixed onto the back that were driven by a second engine. The first, original engine drove the road wheels that actually propelled the Land Rover – the skirt was there simply to take all the weight.

And it would go over anything, particularly exceptionally soft ground that would be likely to bog down a standard Land Rover. Vickers promoted the Hover Rover as an agricultural machine (although the company was keen to get military orders, too) because it was kind to the ground; unlike a tractor, it wouldn't inflict any damage on the surface. But the vehicle couldn't carry anything due to the presence of the second engine and the fans, which somewhat limited its capabilities.

**THE CUTHBERTSON** (see page 19) may look a bit like a tank, but this vehicle actually *is* a tank; well, half a tank. The back end is an Alvis Scorpion – a light tank – that's been grafted onto the front end of a V8 long-wheelbase Land Rover to make a half-track. The idea was to produce a rolling chassis that could then be turned into anything from an ambulance to a missile launcher, or anti-tank gun.

It looks enormous and rather ungainly; although it was extremely good in a straight line off-road, it didn't turn very well. That made it a bit of a handful, a characteristic not helped by the vehicle's seven-tonne fully laden weight. It was also crucifyingly loud inside, pushing 108dB at full speed: very close to unbearable for the human ear. Centaurs suffered from vibration issues and broken driveshafts, too, although it's likely that most of the problems could have been sorted if an army had placed an order. Which, unfortunately, none did, leaving the Centaur to become a real curio – only six of them were ever built.

# INNER BEAUTY

No matter how good a car looks outside, customers spend far more time inside. Here, designers reveal how they rewrote the luxury SUV rulebook with the new Range Rover's cabin

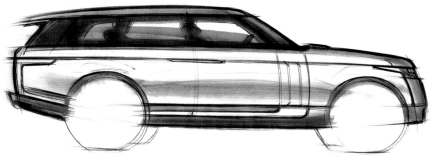

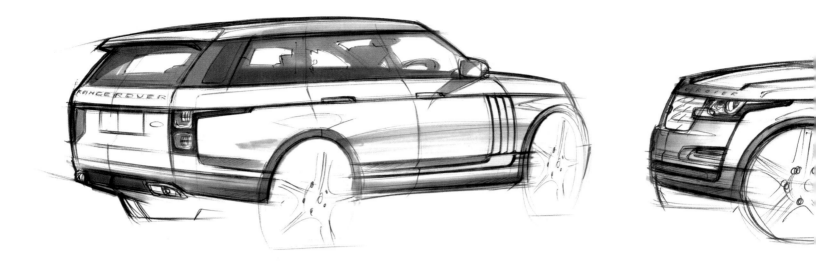

The next time you get into your car, or any car, before getting stuck into the routine of key in the ignition, seatbelt on, feet on pedals, hand on gearlever, give yourself five minutes to think about the interior. Assuming it was designed and built within the last decade, chances are that you'll be sitting in one of the most well engineered, robustly constructed and finely detailed environments in the world. The Space Shuttle's cabin is a touch more safety critical, but it doesn't have to look pretty. The bridge of a Navy destroyer has a lot more functions to fulfil, but it's a bit short on leather-trimmed headlining, where the length of each stitch and the thickness of the thread is as crucial to the result as the actual grain and colour of the leather.

The thing about the brilliant people who create car interiors is that they're not just doing shapes and colours. They're building an environment that moves around, has to be capable of surviving temperatures from plus 40 to minus 40 degrees Celsius and will be used every day for 10, 20 or maybe 30 years. They have to deal with all of those demanding requirements – and that was merely a very short and simple summary. Just wait until we get into crash safety legislation. Then it gets extremely complicated.

And all of this starts with a pen and paper. That's how the new Range Rover's interior began, too: sketches, doodles, ideas and concepts – lines roughed out freehand, long before anyone gets near a computer. Although the essential elements were already in place, as the new car's predecessor had done such a good job of establishing what a Range Rover interior should look like, this model was always going to be something of an evolution.

So that's where they started. Land Rover's interior design manager Nicolas Finney reckons that the old model changed people's perceptions of how wood and leather can (and should) be used in a car. "Before the L322, wood and leather were trim," he says. "The Range Rover changed that." He's talking about the strong structural and architectural look to that car's cabin – how the wood runs under the padded centre section, making it look like it's actually a support structure for the dashboard.

That constructed look has remained, as has the linear layout of the upper, central and lower sections of the dashboard. A large centre console flows from what looks like under the centre of the

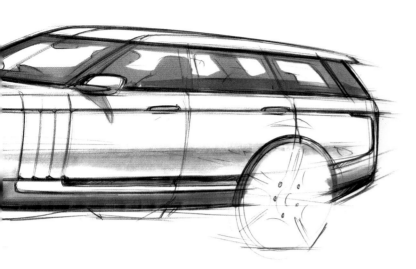

**BELOW, LEFT**
Full-scale mock-ups of proposed interior ideas allow designers to evaluate what will and won't work in the real world

**BELOW, CENTRE**
Early clays of the interior have the fundamentals of the finished cabin, but some details will change, such as the doorhandles

**BELOW, RIGHT**
In the new Range Rover, materials like wood and leather are more than just trim - they've been designed to look like integral components

**BOTTOM, LEFT**
Mood boards help designer Jo Slater (left) to narrow down the selection of materials and colours

**BOTTOM, CENTRE**
Range Rover's cabin has to look and feel great, but it must also serve as a functional and durable environment

**BOTTOM, RIGHT**
Interior proposals are fully trimmed in leather, wood and aluminium, and are indistinguishable from the real thing

**BELOW LEFT**
Panoramic roof
floods the interior
with light. With
the cream leather,
it opens the cabin
up, creating a very
different feel to
an interior trimmed
in black material

**RIGHT**
The massive swathe
of wood that runs
from the rear seats
through the centre
of the car and up
into the centre
console feels
generous and
expensive

**BOTTOM LEFT**
The dials for the
climate control are
made from two types
of plastic, with a
textured finish on
the surface your
fingers will touch.
Painted finish on
the buttons is more
durable than soft-
touch plastics

**BOTTOM CENTRE**
Increasing the
amount of space in
the rear seats was
a key focus for the
new Range Rover's
designers. Many
customers treat
their vehicles as
chauffeur-driven
limousines, so
luxury in the back
is paramount

**BOTTOM RIGHT**
Terrain Response
controls are grouped
together and set in
a sheet of polished
aluminium. Button
count has been kept
to a minimum to
increase the surface
area of the premium
materials in the
cabin, such as this
figured macassar

## "Larger surface areas look more generous, expensive and luxurious"

dashboard, right through the middle of the vehicle. "As a starting point, it was fantastic," says Finney. "We didn't want to reinvent it. We wanted more luxury, as this new Range Rover was moving upmarket, and to concentrate on cutting down on switchgear."

And that, essentially, is a Range Rover interior. As Finney points out, this car has a distinctive interior look. He reckons this is due to all other SUVs being built by car manufacturers. They tend to adapt the look of their car interiors to their SUVs. Land Rover doesn't make saloons, estates or roadsters. It makes 4x4s. So the cabins of Land Rover models don't need to reflect any corporate identity that's been developed for a car rather than an SUV.

The point about cutting down on switches is more important than it first sounds. The finished product has remarkably few surface-mounted buttons and dials – just three rotary controls for the heating, with a selection of small buttons to control the demisters, and a row of switches above them. A couple of switches for the Terrain Response and that's it. Everything else is controlled by the touchscreen in the middle of the dash. And by reducing switches and buttons, you increase the visible surface area, so there's more figured macassar on show, and bigger swathes of piano black. That looks generous, expensive and luxurious.

So that's the starting point. Finney says each designer involved completes hundreds of sketches over three months. The work is then filtered to retain two or three ideas from each member of the team. Among the rational ideas, there'll be a handful of radical proposals. "This is the time to push boundaries," he says. "Often, a couple of those ideas will be developed into full-size clay models, which we show to other departments, so some people outside the design process can see what is, and isn't, a Range Rover interior."

Which brings us to the question of who's in charge – designers or engineers? Because it's all well and good making it look nice, but it has to be built and it has to be durable. "The jobs of designer and engineer seem diametrically opposed," says Finney. "An engineer may do what's been done before, because they know it works, while a designer will want to try something new. But on this project, we had a good rapport, and while there's always a bit of friction, if you argue your case with reason, you'll be understood."

Producing the life-size clay models, which are painted and trimmed in real materials, so they're indistinguishable from a

TFT DIALS

STEERING WHEEL

AUDIO SYSTEM

MATERIAL QUALITY

**MATERIAL QUALITY**
Chunky wood and aluminium give the Range Rover's interior a feeling of great strength and solidity throughout

**AUDIO SYSTEM**
The Range Rover can have up to 29 speakers hidden in the cabin, but you'd be pushed to find them all

**STEERING WHEEL**
The boss is reminiscent of the Evoque's, but the wheel is larger

**TFT DIALS**
Mechanical dials are dispensed with entirely in favour of a TFT screen. The needles sit behind the numbers

**TOUCHSCREEN**
Reducing number of buttons on the dash was a key aim. Screen now incorporates the majority of functions

"You feel your surroundings recede and the cocoon slowly grows around you"

**MIDROLL SECTION**

**TOUCHSCREEN**

**SYMMETRICAL LAYOUT**

**CENTRE CONSOLE**

**COMPARTMENT LID**

**SEATS**

**SYMMETRICAL LAYOUT**
Land Rover considered an off-set, asymmetrical layout, but decided to retain the more formal symmetry

**COMPARTMENT LID**
Designed to retain the impression of a single slab of wood when closed, so as not to break up the continuity

**MIDROLL SECTION**
The idea of a wide horizontal section that divides the cabin is carried over from the previous Range Rover

**CENTRE CONSOLE**
The polished aluminium 'buttresses' give the impression they're integral structural parts

**THE SEATS**
Receive just about more wear than any other interior element, and they're hugely complex, full of fans and motors

# INSPIRED THINKING

Every designer has inspirations, and these objects were the most influential on the Range Rover interior team's thinking. But don't just think of the cabin as a copy – it's the overall look and feel of a piece that the designers take in

> "Wood trim feels thick and solid, like it forms a part of the car's structure"

**LEICA M9**

A design classic that combines cutting-edge digital technology with beautiful materials, and draws on Leica's past without resorting to nasty pastiche

**RIVA AQUARIVA**

A classic fusion of power, elegant proportions and hand-crafted quality. The Riva also had a significant influence on the look of the previous Range Rover's interior

**EAMES LOUNGE CHAIR**

A design icon that's been produced since 1956. The ability to choose lighter leather and veneer combinations has enabled this design to remain absolutely contemporary

real interior, turns a 2D sketch into a 3D reality and improves the understanding across the company of what's trying to be achieved. It's also the point at which the designers know if their ideas are feasible, because now they have to work with hardpoints – fixed positions of items like the gearlever and steering wheel,which are attached to parts of the car you can't see and that can't be moved.

It's also the point at which problems start to appear – such as sorting out the wooden trim sections on either side of the dash top. Because they sit directly underneath the windscreen, they're subjected what engineers call 'high solar loading' – otherwise known as plenty of light and heat. Jo Slater, Land Rover's chief designer for colour, materials and graphics, reckons these pieces of trim were the hardest jobs in the whole cabin: "The solar loading is extremely hard on the wood surfaces," she says.

In fact, if you were to look at it rationally, the whole idea of putting wood and leather in an environment where they're constantly subjected to significant fluctuations in temperature and light is probably a bit daft. If you wanted to make it easy, you'd use more inert materials. Like gold. Although given the weight penalty, plus the fact that even with the Range Rover's move upmarket, the cost might prove off-putting, wood and leather it is.

The wood veneers are bonded to extremely strong substrates, which prevent them from moving around or cracking. That wood is then wrapped over the corners into another plane, which gives each piece of trim a look and feel of thickness and solidity, like it has a purpose and forms an integral part of the car's structure.

Much of what Jo Slater does concerns the combination of durability with amazing looks. So the buttons below the central screen are painted, because soft-touch plastics are, well, too soft. They can also discolour and turn green.

And then there are the seats – a hugely complex element, much more so than the chairs in your house. Because they're able to heat, cool and massage you, they're full of motors, fans, airbags and wiring – all of which have to keep on working in an environment where they can get wet, baked or frozen, or be subjected to many other unpredictable conditions. They're in a car, not someone's sitting room, and cars tend to move around. Fortunately, leather is pretty durable, although like wood, it doesn't respond well to being repetitively heated,

### WALLY SAILING YACHT

Combines exquisite materials with a total essence of form. It's the most radical rethink of what constitutes a sailing yacht, and manages to look beautiful and functional at the same time

### CLEARAUDIO CONCEPT TURNTABLE

Illustrates how high-end audio equipment is visually pared down to a minimum. This simplicity highlights the beauty of the materials used, and emphasises the fantastic attention to detail on each component

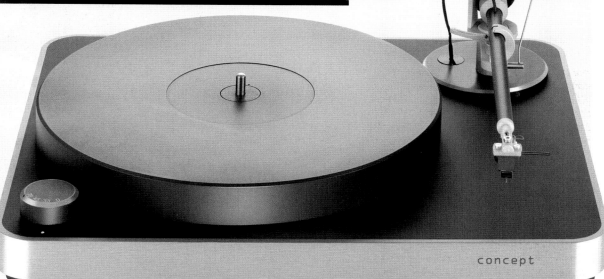

### CLASSIC BRITISH TAILORING

The highest quality clothing is still hand-made by skilled craftsmen, working in a unique British industry that's revered around the world as being the best of its kind

### STAHL HOUSE BY PIERRE KOENIG

A lesson in volume and proportion. The low, elegant, linear form of this house and expansive use of glass highlight the purity and simplicity of its construction

## "Land Rover realised buyers were treating the car as a chauffeur-driven limousine"

cooled and dried. The leather used to trim the new Range Rover's seats is what's known as semi-aniline. It's a two-stage finishing process where the colour is sealed in below a protective coating. Slater says it's been designed so that dirt sits on it rather than sinking into it, making it much easier to clean the seats.

Of course, most Range Rover customers will not know about or notice any of these technical details. But what they most certainly will notice is the spectacular cumulative effect of all these processes, which manifests itself in the form of space, light, symmetry and large, uninterrupted areas of wood, leather and aluminium. Light is actually very important in a Range Rover – the original model featured the most astonishingly airy and glassy cabin, and this latest version carries on that tradition, helped by a monster of a panoramic glass roof.

That glass roof does something more abstract, too. It provides occupants with a visual reminder of the new Range Rover's revolutionary weight-saving aluminium construction, and also expands the driver's and passengers' view out ahead, above and all around the vehicle.

Those occupants should also notice the increased space in the rear. As good as the L322's cabin was, the one thing it didn't quite nail down was rear legroom. This became more of a problem when Land Rover realised that an awful lot of Range Rover buyers were treating the car as a chauffeur-driven limousine, and riding in the back seats. According to Nicolas Finney, the company wasn't quite expecting that, so to chime with this newest model's shift into super-luxury territory, it increased space in the rear and added the option of a set of two individual chairs back there for those who want to recline in luxury.

Finally, you'll notice the calm. Above all, the new Range Rover is supremely relaxing. While threading through brutal, tiresome city traffic on a cold, grey Sunday afternoon, you feel your surroundings recede and the familiar Range Rover cocoon gradually grows around you.

It's a bubble, providing insulation from whatever's going on outside – from the noise, the bustle, the crowds and all of those little irritations that we try so hard to avoid. Aloof? Yes, a little bit. But surely that's a large part of the point, too. "The all-new Range Rover," says Nicolas Finney, "is a sanctuary." LR

**FAR LEFT**
Executive Class
option of individual
chairs instead of a
bench turns the Range
Rover into a limo.
Passengers get their
own climate controls

**LEFT**
Access to the rear is
much better than in
the last Range Rover.
Interior lights
(including the rear
ones) are touch
sensitive

**ABOVE**
Land Rover sells
more Range Rovers
in light interior
colours than darker
ones. It's very
susceptible to
colour changes,
which totally alter
the mood of the cabin

# ORIGIN OF THE SPECIES

After 60 years, the original Land Rover's design lives on in today's models

**FOR A VEHICLE** that has become one of the most recognisable on Earth, it's ironic that the Land Rover was never really designed, not in the modern sense of designing a car. The look was very much created by the need for a simple and quick to build vehicle, led by engineers, not designers. Its construction and the materials used to build it had a very direct and noticeable impact on the way it looked.

It took just one year from the first sketch – drawn on the sand at Red Wharf Bay on Anglesey in April 1947, by Rover's technical director, Maurice Wilks – for the Land Rover to come to fruition. Wilks had a WWII Willys Jeep that he used on his farm, and reckoned that Rover could build something similar, but better. Twelve months later, the Land Rover was launched.

The way that the Land Rover wears its structure on the outside is just one aspect that makes it unique. This was fairly unusual back in 1948, coming as it did when full-width styling – which covered up so much of a car's structure – was making an impact. In contrast, a Series I Land Rover has its hinges on the surface of the door, simply hung into slots on the bulkhead. The earliest Land Rovers don't have an external door handle: you reach through a canvas flap into the cab, which enables you to lift the handle on the inside. It's possible to see the exposed chassis under the bodywork, and you can clearly make out how the bulkhead is bolted to the chassis.

The materials used also make their own contribution to the Land Rover's robust look. Galvanised-steel capping on the tops of the doors and rear body strengthens the panels, and provides an indestructible surface on which to slide items into the vehicle. The windscreen and bumper are made of the same stuff: heavy-duty steel, thickly coated with zinc to prevent it rusting.

The production Land Rover turned out to be more simple than the prototype, which didn't have any doors, but used a more complex rear body. The

**RIGHT**
The centre steer was a prototype testing the concept of a small four-wheel drive. This drawing of the vehicle was commissioned by Land Rover for its 60th anniversary

J. MODEL

LAND ROVER.

PART NO
XI7724

26 LBS

DESCRIPTION :-

| | ALTERATION SUFFIX | | ALTERATION NUMBERS | |
|---|---|---|---|---|
| THE LATEST ALTERATION SUFFIX MUST ALWAYS BE QUOTED AFTER THE PART NUMBER. | ISSUE | DATE | ROVER | CLASS. |
| | | | | |
| | | | | |
| | | | | |

# LAND ROVER

| | | | | | PASSED | THE ROVER CO. LTD. SOLIHULL. |
|---|---|---|---|---|---|---|
| MATERIAL | MATERIAL SPEC! LATEST ISSUE | TREATMENT | BRINELL | WEIGHT | | |

GENERAL ARRANGEMENT OF LAND-ROVER.          SHEET 1/3

CHECKED

DATE   JUNE 47.

PART Nº X17724

J. MODEL       1
LAND ROVER.

DESCRIPTION:-          GENERAL   ARRANGEMENT   OF  LAND-ROVER.          SHEET 1/3

MATERIAL | MATERIAL SPEC LATEST ISSUE | TREATMENT | BRINELL | WEIG

**ABOVE**
Early Land Rover
models employed
strong, robust
materials such as
galvanised steel.
Design was basic:
the doors had no
exterior handles
and the fuel tank
is visible below
the vehicle

**RIGHT**
Rover's Technical
Director, Maurice
Wilks, owned a WWII
Willys Jeep, which
he used on his farm.
He believed that
Rover could build
something better —
and the first Land
Rover was born

## "Arguably, it's the front end of the Land Rover that's changed the least"

sweeping curves of the prototype's front wings were made more upright for the production car, creating a shape that can still be seen on the Defender.

Arguably, it's the front end of the Land Rover that has changed the least. The exposed bonnet hinges, the curved shape of the rear of the bonnet below the windscreen, the relationship of the size and width of the grille to the front wings: all remain pretty much identical to how they were back in 1947.

Again, much of this was driven by function. The shape of the few curved panels was dictated by the requirement to use a minimum of tooling in order to cut costs. The grille and the lights within it were set back to protect the latter from damage (the grille also protects them from stones). You fill the fuel tank – which you can see below the driver's door – by taking out the driver's seat and lifting a lid underneath to access the filler cap. This avoided the need for more holes in the body or a fuel-filler pipe. There's an honesty in the way that a Land Rover looks: the exposed structure, its simplicity – it isn't hiding anything. You really can see what you're getting.

Which, as far as the interior is concerned, isn't very much. A tiny instrument panel holding three dials, a grab handle, three seats and a couple of gear levers: that's your lot. At least the steering wheel is in the right place – the centre steer had it in the middle of the vehicle to avoid having to produce both left- and right-hand-drive models.

So much of this simplification, this reduction to essentials, is strongly reminiscent of the current movement towards building cheap, basic cars such as the Dacia Sandero or Skoda Rapid. Unlike those cars, which are built to a very specific price and designed to offer as much value for money as possible, the Land Rover's simplicity was driven by function.

Of course, the Land Rover has changed a lot in 65 years, and the performance of those very first vehicles is hardly comparable to today's Defender. It was a fundamental change in 1958 that created the look of the current Land Rover, altering the proportions, adding the barrel sides and fixing the hardpoints that haven't really changed. But the intent of the first Land Rovers – the idea of the world's most versatile vehicle, as the advertising of the time put it – very much lives on. **LR**

**ABOVE, TOP**
The name of 1947's Centre Steer prototype derived from its steering wheel, located in the centre of the vehicle. The design is still unmistakably Land Rover

**ABOVE, CENTRE**
New styling cues for the Series II Land Rover in 1958 included curved body sides, which replaced the flat sides of previous models

**ABOVE, BOTTOM**
The exterior design of the current Defender – including the distinctive bonnet shape and upright wings — is strongly influenced by earlier models

# LAND ROVER
# THE JOURNEY

Land Rovers have discovered, explored and unearthed some of the remotest and wildest places on Earth. And every one is built and designed as a true off-roader

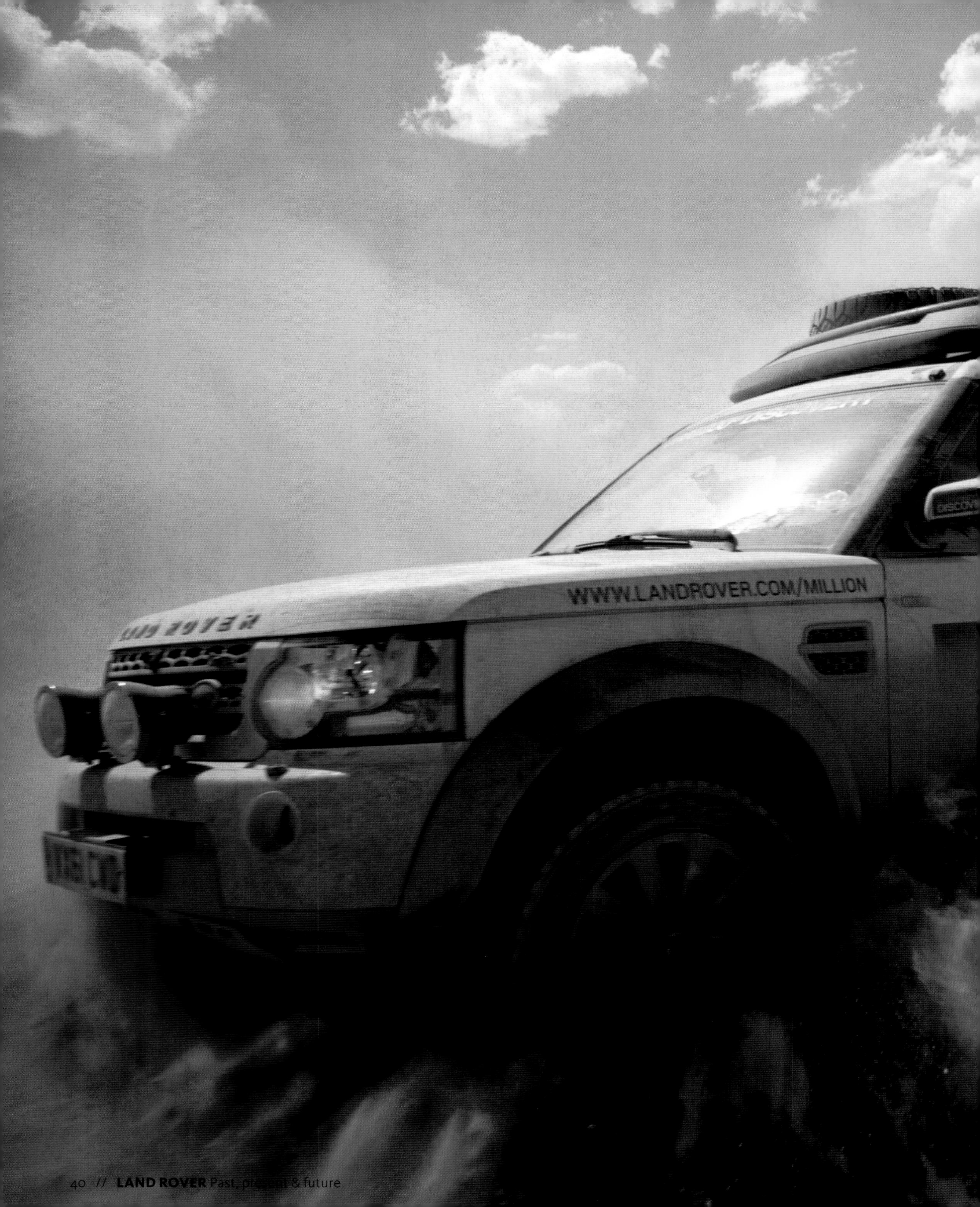
WWW.LANDROVER.COM/MILLION

# ORIENT EXPRESS

Jack Rix joins a quartet of Discoverys – including the millionth model to roll off the production line – as they head out on an epic, 10,000-mile overland expedition to China with a strict Beijing Show deadline

# A

**AROUND 35 MINUTES** into the journey I clock the sheer absurdity of my situation – I'm slumped in the back of a 30-year-old Volkswagen Santana, heading down a nondescript motorway to I-have-no-idea-where. My driver is trying his very best to spark up a conversation, but his lack of English and my ignorance of Mandarin are proving to be a sticking point. Come to think of it, it's remarkable that I decided to climb into this stranger's car at all: he had no plaque bearing my name to welcome me, and no obvious affiliation with Land Rover. What he *did* have was an ability to point vigorously at his taxi, which – at that bewildering moment when you step out of the airport onto alien soil – was apparently enough for me.

More confusion: we've arrived at a vast petrol station, and the driver is now out of the car and gesturing wildly. I wind down the window, poke my head out and tell him in my clearest Queen's English that I absolutely have no money and no intention of paying for his petrol. He's recruited the pump attendant by this point, who joins in with the mime act; so I deliver the same message again, only this time with more force. At that point a local street trader calmly wanders over and translates: "You need to get out and wait – he can't have passengers while filling the car." I make my apologies and meekly hop out.

Fifty miles further up the road and I'm resigned to the fact that I might never reach my destination, and could well die of heat exhaustion on this beige velour back seat. So when we climb a gentle incline and the barren, parched landscape transforms instantly into a sandy desert in front of us, I don't take much notice. But after glancing out of the back window, my jaw hits the floor. A definite, arrow-straight line bisects the countryside where sand meets dirt: the land is lapping onto a gargantuan beach. Finally we pull over, I'm transferred into a 4x4 and we clamber over the dunes to our hotel, which stands alone in the golden wilderness. It's then that the scale of China sinks in.

I'm here to take the baton for the final leg of Land Rover's Journey of Discovery from Birmingham to Beijing, but it might as

**BELOW**
Aside from a few accessories that you can buy from a dealer, the expedition cars are totally standard

**ABOVE**
The mountains of the Ala-Archa national park in Kyrgyzstan were open only to the Soviet elite until the early nineties

**RIGHT**
Even a Land Rover can't go everywhere – sometimes you have to travel by helicopter, especially if you need to get to the top of a mountain

"Glancing out of the rear window, my jaw hits the floor. There's a definite line where sand hits dirt: the land is lapping onto a gargantuan beach"

**TOP**
The Discoverys get put through their paces even before leaving Europe. Here, the team get to show off their dune-busting abilities on an off-road course just outside Vienna

**ABOVE LEFT**
Camping on the road can throw up some fine sights, including this breathtaking sunset

**ABOVE RIGHT**
Bounding through sand dunes isn't necessarily sensible on a 10,000-mile journey, but it's definitely fun

"There can be no better test of a car's reliability, durability and long-distance abilities than an epic journey such as this"

well be the 4 x 100m Olympic final – you could say that I'm feeling the pressure. Why? Because on 29 February 2012, four identical Discoverys – including the millionth Discovery ever to roll off the line – embarked on an incredible 10,000-mile road trip, from the car's birthplace at the Solihull plant to China. My job is to bring them over the line in one piece: an 800-mile, two-day jaunt from the desert in Zhongwei to Beijing.

There can be no better test of a car's reliability, durability and long-distance abilities than pitting it against the globe on an epic journey such as this. It's the exact kind of expedition that the Discovery was designed for, right from its very conception; and if there was the opportunity to have some fun and celebrate the milestone of this millionth model along the way, then so much the better. There's a specific reason for ending up in China, too. Not only was the plan to arrive in Beijing just days before the Motor Show rolled into town, but it was also to celebrate the ever-evolving success story between Land Rover and the country with the world's fastest-growing economy.

Over the past few years, the rise of Jaguar and Land Rover sales in China has been astronomical. It's now JLR's largest market, with 71,940 vehicles sold in 2012 from a total of 357,773; this represents a staggering 70 per cent growth. Twenty per cent of all the cars that JLR builds are now exported to China, and new dealerships are currently being opened at a rate of one a week.

By the time that I meet the crew of Land Rover Experience experts, the core team have been on the road for 48 days, passed through 13 countries and tackled every type of terrain, from snow drifts to deserts. After the entire Solihull workforce had waved off the convoy in a glittering ceremony from within the bowels of the factory itself, the cars found their feet on the smooth roads into Geneva, for a photo-call at the Geneva Motor Show. There, the appeal to raise £1m for the International Federation of Red Cross and Red Crescent Societies was launched in front of the world's media.

Pleasantries exchanged, the convoy headed west into the meat of Europe and towards two remarkable landmarks in Ukraine, far from the well-beaten track. It took an hour and a half of document checking before the cars were allowed inside the 30km exclusion zone around Chernobyl. Here the crew met Valeriy, one of the

**RIGHT**
Mikhail Krasinets'
fabulous collection
of more than 400
Soviet-era cars
lies just south of
Moscow. Although
the exhibits are
hardly in pristine
condition, there
is an example from
every year of
production for every
major Russian car
manufacturer. It
stands as testament
to an often-ignored
chapter of global
motoring history

"The convoy headed west into the meat of Europe and towards two remarkable landmarks in Ukraine"

## SECRET SUBMARINE BASE
### BALAKLAVA, UKRAINE

This extraordinary underground submarine base remained operational until 1993; it was designed to be indestructible, even in the event of a direct nuclear blast. It's now open to the public, and is a fascinating and stark reminder of the Cold War

**RIGHT**
The things you can get away with when you're doing something for charity: the convoy gets special permission to pose for a picture or two in the middle of Moscow's Red Square

**LEFT**
10th-century mud-brick walls of Itchan Kala in Khiva, Usbekistan, are a UNESCO World Heritage site and a fine backdrop for a now-dusty troupe of Land Rovers as they head towards China

fearless men who risked their lives hosing down the reactor immediately after the disaster in 1986; only six of them are still alive. The subsequent visit to a nuclear submarine base hidden among the rocky coastline was a less emotional experience, I'm told, but no less awe-inspiring – the metal doors are six metres thick, mighty enough to withstand the power of a nuclear blast.

After feeding the cars on low-grade unleaded in Kazakhstan, and making it to the border with Uzbekistan with minutes to spare before it shut for the night, the crew were greeted by roads riddled with gaping potholes. This meant even earlier starts and later finishes to ensure that they kept within the schedule. And then, days before the cars were due to cross into China, the only border point was blocked by mudslides. Thanks to bulldozers shovelling dirt through the night, the convoy clambered over the terrain and just made it through. After a few days' driving through the Xinjiang province, the cars arrived at the same hotel where they were told I would be waiting for them. Against all the odds, I was.

If the crew hadn't recalled their personal highs and lows to me that night over a warming bowl of catfish and cabbage, you would never have known what these intrepid Discoverys had been through. The only technical problems that the team had encountered were a couple of punctures and several stone chips thanks to Uzbekistan's crumbling roads; remarkable when you consider that the cars are entirely standard. Powered by 5.0-litre petrol V8s – diesel is scarce in remote areas – all four were fitted with roof racks to carry jerry cans of fuel and spare tyres, and clad with underbody protection for the worst terrain. But nothing was added that you or I couldn't order from a Land Rover dealer.

My first day behind the wheel begins at 6.30am, as we head east at speed on a newly built and deserted motorway heading arrow-straight through the apocalyptic landscape. Our sat-nav

**RIGHT**
The border crossing into China is the start of the last leg and though the cars may be dirty, they haven't missed a beat

**RIGHT**
With 10,000 miles of grime covering them, the four Discoverys are a little more grubby than the rest of the Beijing show's gleaming metal

**ABOVE**
After some of the rough roads the Discoverys tackled in the former Soviet states, smooth Chinese Tarmac is a welcome sight

**TOP RIGHT**
Uzbekistan is pretty remote in places; this ancient hill fort clearly doesn't get all that many visitors

**BOTTOM RIGHT**
Before heading into the motor show exhibition centre there's a brief chance to play the tourist with a trip to Tiananmen Square

## "As we pull up outside the hotel, you could be forgiven for thinking that we'd simply popped to the local shops"

confidently tells us that there's more than 1100km to cover; fortunately this is a temporary blip, as it soon recalculates and 400km is chopped from the total. China is building new roads at such a rapid rate that drivers have to update their sat-nav software every three months – in Europe, once a year is enough.

After miles of flat, rural scenery, pebble-smooth Tarmac and misspelled road signs urging drivers to 'Buckly Up', we hit upon a traffic jam that makes the M25 at rush hour seem quiet. For a grand total of 12 miles we sweep past hundreds of coal trucks, all of which are obediently parked nose to tail on the inside lane, while women with baskets of sweets harass the drivers for their spare change. Eventually we pass the cause of the jam: a snarled-up coal truck has made contact with the barrier and now lies strewn across the road. Our guide tells us that the law dictates that, when something like this occurs, the truckers – who carry a third of all China's coal along this Tsing Tao expressway – are duty-bound to keep right and allow the faster traffic to flow past.

Our overnight stay is in the 'small' town of Taiyuan: it's actually home to more than four million people, and is a jumbled metropolis containing little besides bad drivers and a general clamour. It is therefore with some relief that we find ourselves needing to leave early the following morning, with just 300 miles now standing between us and Beijing. But negotiating Chinese roads, and Chinese drivers, is far from straightforward. The rule is to expect the worst and stay alert. Cars making unpredictable lane changes, road sweepers in the outside lane and unmarked roadworks are just some of the hazards that the Discoverys find themselves needing to dance around.

Undeterred by the kamikaze traffic, fog and drizzle we make a bee-line for Beijing, and cross the city limits around lunchtime. As we pull up outside our hotel and toss the keys to another crew responsible for delivering the cars to the Beijing show stand (dirt and all), you could be forgiven for thinking that we'd simply popped to the shops, rather than traversed 10,000 miles across the globe. Both the absence of damage to the vehicles and lack of fatigue on the faces of those driving are testament to the Discoverys' phenomenal breadth of talents. We set out with the intention of completing the trip to China; in the end, we could have driven from Birmingham to Beijing – and back. LR

# IN THE FOOTSTEPS OF PIONEERS

How the Journey of Discovery was inspired by the story of six young men who made expedition history

In 1955, six students from Oxford and Cambridge Universities set out in a pair of Series One Land Rovers on the Oxford and Cambridge Far Eastern Expedition – now known as the First Overland Expedition. Sponsored primarily by Land Rover – which provided the vehicles – but also by other independent contributions of cash and equipment, the trip captured the public's imagination. It was the first time that vehicles of this type had attempted such a route, and it was the last recorded car journey along the Ledo road from India to Burma: shortly after, the border between the two countries was closed.

The students set off from London's Hyde Park and intended to end up in Beijing, but were forced to change their destination to Singapore due to political reasons. In total, the trip took six months and six days, and covered 18,000 miles. The Land Rovers were, by the standards of today, agricultural – leaf springs, four-speed gearboxes, no power steering and simple seats – but in the mid-1950s they were as good as a four-wheel-drive car could get. Even so, the concept of covering 18,000 miles in one is daunting.

The trip inspired a BBC documentary narrated by Sir David Attenborough, which can still be found on YouTube; a book called *First Overland* by expedition member Tim Slessor was published two years after the journey's triumphant conclusion.

The Oxbridge students' 1955 route was definitely well off the beaten path - cars were not a common sight across this bridge

How things change. In the mid-1950s this photo location near the Aral Sea would have been well under water

The original trip went through Iran and Burma, a route impossible to take in 2012. But back in the fifties the team had intended to finish in Beijing and were only stopped by political tensions, while China welcomed the 2012 Discovery convoy with open arms

**PRESENT-DAY ROUTE**

BIRMINGHAM

MOSCOW

LONDON

PARIS

BEIJING

GENEVA

ANKARA

DUNHUANG

TEHRAN

LAHORE

**ORIGINAL ROUTE**

NEPAL

LAOS

BANGKOK

KUALA LUMPUR

JAKARTA

Technology may have come a long way, but as the modern Journey of Discovery proves, it is still possible to get yourself stuck

It was a case of leaf springs, no power steering and no electronic aids for the First Overland drivers, but the Series I Land Rover was a capable companion

Today's Land Rover Discovery is full of creature comforts, but its go-anywhere capability is still there should you want to make use of it

Seven decades ago, the idea of leather-seats, air-con or iPad-compatible stereos would have seemed like science fiction for the driver of a rugged early Land Rover

The Journey of Discovery convoy approach their Chinese finish line having collected little more than a solid coating of dust and grime along the way

If there's no road, then sometimes you just have to build one with whatever materials are available to you

# THE BIGGER PICTURE

Celebrating the abilities of the new Range Rover and the Defender with some of the finest images of these two iconic vehicles on and off-road

## RANGE ROVER WITH AIRSTREAM
### ATLAS MOUNTAINS, MOROCCO

Two icons - the Range Rover and the classic
Airstream trailer - negotiate a mountain road
in the Atlas Mountains. The idea of towing an
Airstream to Morocco was concocted as part of
the new Range Rover's launch programme

## MILITARY 110
**LONGMOOR TRAINING CAMP, SURREY**
In the right hands, a coil-sprung Land Rover
is pretty much unstoppable off-road, even
in the claggy clay mud of this Army off-road
course. Narrow tyres with an aggressive tread
pattern help the Land Rover cut through the
mud to find something solid underneath. And
no, you wouldn't normally stop halfway through
climbing a hill like this, but the shot was
too good to miss...

## DEFENDER 90
### EASTNOR CASTLE

If there's one location outside Solihull that can claim to be Land Rover's second home, it's Eastnor Castle in Herefordshire. The firm has been off-road testing its vehicles here since 1961 and a significant proportion of every new model's development is carried out at the estate. Here, a Defender ploughs through a deep water channel on the estate.

It looks as at home in the wilderness of the Moroccan desert as it does outside the Royal Albert Hall - the Range Rover has always done dual-purpose with ease. Its extensive off-road ability comes from the long-travel suspension - the rear wheels will move more than 110mm more than any rival's - cross-linked air suspension to keep all the tyres in contact with the ground, an optional locking rear differential and the new Terrain Response system. It automatically selects the right setting for the kind of ground you're crossing, and it will wade through 900mm of water, 200mm deeper than the last model.

### DEFENDER 110
#### AMAZON JUNGLE
Back in the early nineties, the Camel Trophy was up there with the Dakar Rally as the toughest off-road adventure in the world. The 1989 event crossed the Amazon jungle, on a route believed to be impassable during the rainy season. Which was when the event took place. Here, a 110 is being winched out of the huge washout it has fallen into.

### DEFENDER 110
**PACKINGTON FORD, WARWICKSHIRE**

A Defender immersed in deep water on a flooded road near the firm's Solihull base. This depth of water doesn't generally present much of an obstacle to a Defender, and fitting a raised air intake allows it go deeper. Developing a bow wave at the front keeps water away from the engine compartment by creating a trough around the vehicle.

Land Rover chose Morocco as the venue for the
Range Rover launch because it offered a mix of
good Tarmac for on-road driving and unbeatable
off-roading. And in 1970 the original Range
Rover was going to be launched there, but at the
last minute Rover changed its mind and chose
Cornwall instead. Here the Range Rover
sits in front of the astonishing backdrop of
the Atlas Mountains as the sun goes down.

# RECOVERY

Early in 2013, Land Rover helped a team of injured servicemen take on a daunting new challenge: to complete

# VEHICLES

the infamous Dakar Rally, the world's most gruelling off-road race. Here's their incredible story

We're in a dusty bivouac in Calama, Chile, when word reaches us: the Wildcat of Ben Gott and double-amputee Mark Zambon has had an accident, rolling out of the sixth stage of the 2013 Dakar Rally. For the Race2Recovery team, it's yet another painful moment in what has already proved to be a fraught week. The Dakar is the self-styled 'toughest rally in the world', but during the first week three of the four Defender-based Wildcats have retired, and last night a trio of support crew were involved in an horrific road-traffic accident.

Race2Recovery was the brainchild of Captain Tony Harris and Corporal Tom Neathway. Both were blown up while serving in Afghanistan, and they met at Headley Court, a rehabilitation centre in Surrey. Harris had lost his left leg below the knee, while Neathway lost his legs and an arm. Both were after a challenge. "It's about getting back that adrenaline rush," says Neathway, "while showing other injured service personnel that anything is possible."

What began as a bar-room chat morphed into a 28-strong organisation with backing from big corporations including Land Rover, which donated Discoverys as support vehicles and helped train the team. Even reaching the start of the race had been an epic achievement; now the goal was to finish.

But the journey didn't begin well. Before the first stage, Harris and co-driver Cathy Derousseaux suffered a broken differential. He attempted the stage in two-wheel drive, got stuck and didn't make it back for hours. On the second stage, the fan belt snapped and they had to wait for the support truck.

Harris started the following stage and completed it. But after analysing the previous day, the organisers excluded them for missing waypoints and they had to retire a healthy car. Two days later, the Wildcat of Neathway and driver Justin Birchall would also be out. Scaling a dune in the dark, they suffered terminal damage to their gearbox and transfer case.

Back to the present day, and the team is facing another crisis. It's gone midnight, one of the two remaining Wildcats has had an accident and the other is still out in the wilds. Now Major Matthew O'Hare and Corporal Philip 'Barney' Gillespie have until tomorrow morning to make it back to the bivouac, or Race2Recovery's mission will be over.

A year ago, O'Hare's off-road driving experience amounted to little more than kerb-hopping his Fiat Panda in London, but now he's taking on a 5500-mile rally across South America with an amputee co-driver who's also a novice. The car they're driving has suffered a few issues, too. Christened 'Joy', it broke down twice on the way to the start line. Then it developed an oil leak before the rally had even begun. Then it started overheating.

But after four welcome hours of sleep, we're met by some good news: co-driver Mark Zambon has been given the all-clear following that accident and is back with the team. Zambon, a US Marine, worked as a bomb-disposal technician and had been blown up four times when a fifth explosion removed his legs. Now he'd just rolled out of the Dakar. "We hit a ditch at about 60mph," he explains. "Then we went boom; the windscreen flew about 30 yards." A Dutch race truck stopped to help. "When one of the guys pulled me out, one of my legs fell off and he panicked. I was shouting

"The journey didn't begin well: the team suffered a broken differential before the first stage"

**TOP LEFT AND ABOVE**
Captain Tony Harris and co-driver Cathy Derousseaux crossing the rally start-line in Lima; Harris sets to work on his Wildcat after the car suffered a broken differential before the first stage

**LEFT**
Triple amputee Tom Neathway lost his limbs after stepping on a booby trap in Afghanistan, during 2008. Race2Recovery was the brainchild of Neathway and Tony Harris

**FAR LEFT**
The Race2Recovery campaign in Dakar encompassed a 28-strong team of drivers, co-drivers, mechanics and other support staff. The race began in Peru, and travelled via Argentina to Chile

'prosthetic', but he didn't understand. Yesterday was the second anniversary of when I was blown up. Maybe on the next anniversary I'll stay in bed."

We're told that Joy is on her way. Then, with Hollywood timing, she bursts into the bivouac, completes a U-turn and heads straight back out again. There's no time for a proper service. How are they keeping going? Gillespie's hair and face are layered in dust and his eyes are red. "I don't know, mate," he says. "Matt's incredible." He's been wearing his prosthetic limb for almost three days, something that the doctors discourage; his stump is swollen and painful.

They get through stage seven and into Argentina, on tracks more akin to the World Rally Championship than the Dakar. The dunes are over for now and, against the odds, Team Joy makes it to the rest day.

For team manager Pav Taylor, this marks the end of phase two. Phase one was getting to the start; phase three is about making it to the finish. Taylor was seriously injured by a suicide bomber in Afghanistan and is the rock upon which Race2Recovery is built. This week he's barely slept, has had to extricate injured friends from a vehicle and rescue a Wildcat in the dead of night.

On the rest day, the mechanics replace Joy's radiators and fashion a makeshift cooling system from a water spray and a sponge. All hope now rests on this one car and its novice crew. There's still more than 2000 miles to go, and the support truck has retired. If Joy breaks down or gets stuck, they'll have to rely on their wits or help from other teams.

But the following day is the rally's longest: 852km, with a 593km special stage. It's also the hottest. Midnight passes and then, as the clock strikes one, there's the familiar cry of a Wildcat V8. "Joy hasn't overheated once, we've actually been overtaking other cars," yells O'Hare. "It's a fantastic feeling."

By now, more than a third of the competition has dropped out; many that remain are a sorry sight. But Team Joy is keeping it together. They're last, but the dream of making the finish is still alive. "Every time I'm down, I think of the charity," says O'Hare. The mission is to raise money for the Personal Recovery Centre at Tedworth House, which treats injured servicemen.

And then, on 19 January 2013, Philip 'Barney' Gillespie crosses the line to become the first amputee to complete the Dakar. "I've been through some dark times," he says at the finish. "I hope I've shown to other injured people that life isn't over and that you can achieve extraordinary things."

Lesser men would not have faced up to such a ridiculous mix of challenges, but Race2Recovery was founded on extraordinary courage. As Neathway put it, "we've known worse." By their own admission, O'Hare is not the world's finest rally driver or Gillespie the finest co-driver, but they fully deserve their place in Dakar – and motorsport – history. LR

**TOP, LEFT**
The Race2Recovery faced some challenges that most rally crews just wouldn't have to deal with; here, a prosthetic leg is adjusted

**ABOVE**
Team Joy completed the race, piloted by Major Matt O'Hare (pictured, top left) and Corporal Philip Gillespie (top right)

**BELOW**
The jubilant
Race2Recovery team
welcome their car
across the line at
the finish of the
Dakar Rally. The race
covers more than 5000
miles and takes two
weeks to complete

"More than a third of the cars have dropped
out, and many that remain look a sorry sight"

# LOCH & ROLL

Mike Duff braves below-zero temperatures to take on Land Rover Experience's vast
Blair Atholl off-road course, in a true multi-terrain test of the Freelander's abilities

# THE

LOCH REFLECTS the steel-grey colour of the angry sky above. The wind is rising, scudding the water's surface into sizeable waves that slap themselves against the rocky shore. They send spray onto a line of windswept trees as the sub-zero temperatures freeze the water into cascades of icicles. On each side, the loch is framed by snow-covered hills, with grey, distant mountains completing the almost impossibly scenic backdrop. It's pretty much the Highlands cliché that you'd expect to find on a tin of shortbread.

This is Loch Ordie on the vast Atholl estate in Tayside. We're five miles from the nearest paved road and a thousand feet above sea level. The snow that's been falling for most of the morning has stopped, giving us a chance to appreciate the splendour of the landscape, but it'll soon return. It's the sort of view that, ordinarily, you'd have to get extremely cold to see in all its majesty.

The thought of just how cold makes me shiver, so I reach down and turn the Freelander's heated seats up to their warmest setting. Then I tweak the blower fan a couple of notches for good measure, feeling the blast of heat swirl around my completely dry boots. Adventure shouldn't really be this easy - should it?

Since the brand's foundation in 1948, Land Rovers have been designed to go where other, more ordinary cars can't. Proper off-road ability is still regarded as crucial for any car that wears the badge. But just how far into the wilderness can an ordinary production Land Rover get? To find out, we've brought a Freelander to the Atholl estate, which is home to the Scottish Land Rover Experience, to see what even the entry-level model is capable of.

The weather clearly didn't think that the Atholl estate's expanse of moor and mountain offered enough of a challenge – how else to explain the heavy fall of snow and the blizzard conditions promised later on? This is set to be a proper trip into the unknown – even our Land Rover Experience guide for the day, Will, admits he doesn't know what conditions are going to be like higher up in the hills. Our Freelander is a 2.2 SD4 HSE in standard spec, with mud- and snow-rated tyres rather than the pure snow versions we'd probably have chosen for the Arctic conditions. Let's hope they're up to the challenge.

First, there's orientation for both the Freelander and myself – meaning a chance to go and play on the Land Rover Experience's obstacle course. This has been designed to show off the fairly amazing things that Land Rovers can do in terms of ground clearance and axle articulation, but also to teach drivers how to cope with the challenges they'll face in the wilderness proper.

I'm certainly no off-road veteran, but I've been to similar places before, including an amazing day at the company's Eastnor Castle test site years ago. It never ceases to amaze me what a Land Rover is capable of scrambling its way over, through, or sometimes even under if you know what you're doing. It'll tackle obstacles that most able-bodied people would struggle to conquer

"This is set to be a proper trip into the unknown – even our guide admits that he doesn't know what conditions will be like"

**ABOVE**
Ground clearance
is class-leading
when compared
with that of its
competitors

**TOP LEFT**
With the Freelander,
The Land Rover name
took on a new breed
of road-biased small
SUVs, but without
losing its off-road
credibility

**TOP RIGHT**
The Freelander has
a kerbweight of just
1805kg, meaning that
it can tackle softer
ground than its
bigger siblings

**ABOVE**
Weaving through
the trees at the
Scottish Land Rover
Experience Centre
- one of 10 in the UK

"Even by the gargantuan standards of most Highland estates, Blair Atholl is a biggie"

At 145,000 acres, the Atholl estate is seven times the size of Manhattan. That makes it really easy to get lost, particularly in poor weather

**ABOVE, TOP**
The Atholl estate
course consists of
dips and gullies,
towering piles of
earth, a water splash
and an unforgiving
cross-axle test

**ABOVE, BOTTOM**
Our standard
Freelander was
fitted with mud-
and-snow tyres,
which coped
admirably with the
tricky conditions

## "It's a cardinal sin to drive through standing water quick enough to splash the bonnet"

on foot. Which is where instructor Will comes in, giving instructions from the passenger seat or – when things get extremely sticky – from outside via radio.

Although it's the cheapest model in the range, the Freelander has certainly been designed to work off-road. It doesn't have a low-range gearbox, used to multiply the engine's torque at low speed and help you scramble over stuff. Instead, it uses clever stability control, in conjunction with four-wheel drive, to keep you rolling when things become slippery. There's also the reassurance of Land Rover's Hill Descent Control, which helps maintain a set speed down steep descents. While the Freelander can't match the ground clearance of the Discovery or Range Rover, it's class-leading when compared with 'soft roaders' from other manufacturers. And it's got one trick that could prove decisive in the slippery conditions: at 1805kg it's a mere waif compared with its bigger siblings, so should pass over softer ground easily without bogging down.

Before I'm let out on the estate, I've got to prove that I'm up to the centre's various obstacles. These include dips and gullies carved out of the ground, as well as towering piles of earth that require you to inch your way forwards and upwards at 45 degrees, while looking at nothing but sky. There's a water splash that would cover the roof of an ordinary car, plus the star attraction: a wicked cross-axle test. This is made up of a pair of 40-degree side slopes in opposite directions – any vehicle that passes between them has to make its way forward using just three wheels, as the front and rear axles are deflected in different directions. Even more exciting is when the car tips from one side to the other, the entire weight of the vehicle momentarily balanced on the two wheels that remain in contact with the earth. The Freelander passes with flying colours, its stability-control system twanging and chattering as it uses the brakes to stop the wheels from spinning uselessly in the air.

The Centre is a test of the driver as much as the car, and a chance for me to brush up on my off-road skills. It's also good to reacquaint myself with the Land Rover way of tackling challenging terrain: slow, steady and in control. Attacking the wilderness at full throttle might seem like fun, but it massively increases the risk of damaging the car, its occupants or both. Will informs me that it's regarded as a cardinal sin to drive through standing water quickly enough to splash the bonnet – "you've no idea what's in there, have you?"

Throughout the morning, the lessons start to sink in as the Freelander and I grind our way around the challenging course, until Will reckons I'm ready to be unleashed on the considerably greater challenge of the estate itself.

Even by the gargantuan standards of most Highland estates, Atholl is a biggie. At 145,000 acres – 226 square miles if you'd prefer – it's barely smaller than Birmingham, Manchester and Edinburgh combined. That offers plenty

**LEFT**
The Freelander's
advanced off-road
features include
Hill Descent
Control, stability
control and a Terrain
Response System

The landscape of
the Atholl estate is
bleak but beautiful,
and it even has its
own private army

## THE LAND ROVER EXPERIENCE EXPLAINED

Land Rover has always recognised that off-road success means training drivers as well as building cars with the raw capabilities to cope off-road. And the Land Rover Experience has become one of the best ways to do that.

Started in 1990, the idea was to provide owners of the then just-launched Discovery with some idea what their vehicles were capable of. Many were new to not only Land Rover but also to four-wheel drives and off-roading, so Land Rover decided to teach them what to do. It also had the advantage of reducing warranty costs because owners knew how not to damage their cars.

There are now 10 Land Rover Experience centres in the UK, and another 13 across the world, as far afield as Guangzhou in China and Hämeeenlinna in Finland, with each offering the chance to test yourself and to sample the current range of Land Rovers off-road. And they do on-road training, and train professional drivers for the likes of the Highays Agency and Mountain Rescue teams. The instructors are experts, often with huge experience of global off-road adventures. Every level is catered for, from beginners to experienced drivers looking to hone their skills.

"I don't need our guide, Will, to tell me that if we stop we're unlikely to start again"

of opportunities to get lost and, of course, stuck. The Atholl estate even has its own army: uniquely within Europe, the Duke of Atholl retains the right to recruit his own private force – the Atholl Highlanders – to act as his ceremonial bodyguard. That should help with the size of any search party, at least.

Getting onto the estate means leaving the small town of Dunkeld on a lane and passing through a series of gates. We're soon on a snow-covered track heading north. The going is bumpy and slippery, but the Freelander copes well; the 'grass, gravel and snow' setting on the Terrain Response System doing an excellent job of extracting traction. At right, there's the brooding outline of Deuchary Hill, its flank formed from an alternating pattern of white snow and what appears to be black forest. At 1670 feet above sea level, it's a minnow by Highland standards, but it's big enough to dominate the skyline.

We skirt around the hill at a cautious pace, enjoying both the spectacular views and the Freelander's powerful heater. The car takes the track in its stride, only the occasional sunken patch providing even a slight challenge as the bumpers rub against the heather. Until now, there have been clear wheel marks to follow, but when we pass the cottages that the track leads to, we find ourselves on fresh, virgin snow. A new challenge emerges: working out which way to go. Only the slightest indentations show where the track lies beneath the snow; as such, our concentration levels rise and our speed falls.

Loch Ordie is spectacular, and we stop for photographs before carrying on to what Will promises will be a far more challenging track. And so it proves, with the need to traverse an area that flooding has turned into something closely approximating a bog. It takes the Freelander a couple of seconds to break through the frozen surface, into the dark mud underneath. Immediately I feel resistance build while our momentum falls – and I don't need Will to tell me that if we stop we're unlikely to be able to start again. Instinctively, I floor the throttle; in an old-fashioned off-roader, that would be a mistake, spinning the wheels and digging us into the mire. But the Freelander's traction control works out what's necessary and applies just enough extra gas to keep us moving; it gets us to the other side, muddy but unbowed. And then, with perfect timing, the snow properly starts to fall. It's time to head back to base.

So how does a Freelander cope in the wild? As well as we'd hoped, all told. If I'd tried harder then I'm sure that I could have found an obstacle that would have got us properly stuck. But that's not how real off-road driving works: if you don't get home in one piece, then you've failed. The Freelander proved to be more than up to the challenge of taking on some of the wildest terrain in the UK, as well as coping with several inches of snow. On that basis, it's proved itself adventure-rated, as far as I'm concerned.

**LEFT**
The 'grass, gravel and snow' setting on the Freelander 2's Terrain Response System made easy work of the Blair Atholl off-road course

**TOP LEFT AND MIDDLE**
Despite its mainstream family car design brief and monocoque chassis, the Freelander is thoroughly at home getting muddy over rough terrain

**ABOVE**
Water obstacles should be driven through slowly enough to avoid splashing the bonnet, in case of invisible rocks or potholes beneath the surface

REDEFINE THE POSSIBLE

We expect more from digital music.

Meridian's award-winning resolution enhancement technologies
now in a smart, portable form. Appreciate the purest sound
from any computer for headphone or HiFi listening.

**meridian-audio.com**

# LAND ROVER
# INNOVATION

The world's best in-car sound system, the world's most advanced aluminium factory, the world's first SUV – Land Rover has never stopped innovating and developing in 65 years

# HOW TO MAKE THE WORLD'S BEST IN-CAR AUDIO SYSTEM

High-end audio brand Meridian makes some of the best home sound systems you can buy. And now it's brought its expertise to the latest Range Rover models

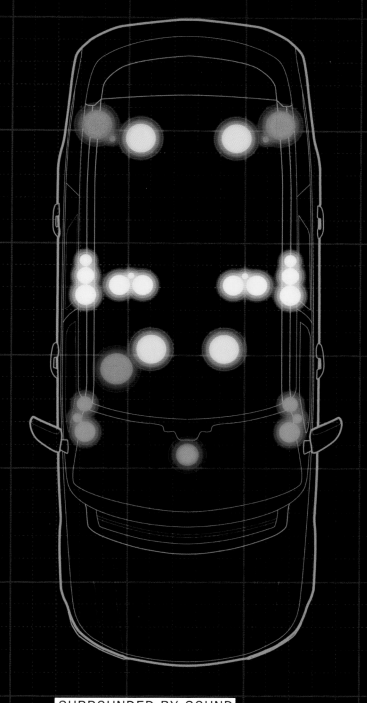

**TRUNK TRIM**
100mm polypropylene
cone midrange
25mm aluminium dome
tweeter

**ROOF LINING**
80mm glass midrange

**FRONT SEATBACK**
2x 80mm glass fibre
midrange
1x 25mm titanium
tweeter

**REAR DOORS**
200mm polypropylene
cone woofer
100mm polypropylene
cone midrange
25mm aluminium dome
tweeter

**FRONT DOORS**
200mm polypropylene
cone woofer
100mm polypropylene
cone midrange
25mm aluminium dome
tweeter

**CENTRE DASH TOP**
100mm polypropylene
cone midrange
25mm aluminium dome
tweeter

**UNDER SEAT**
250mm glass fibre /
pulp cone subwoofer

## SURROUNDED BY SOUND
A total of 29 speakers go to make up the Range Rover's
clever 3D sound system - a world-first for a car

**PSYCHOACOUSTICS.** It's a real thing. A science, no less – the study of the psychological and physiological responses to sounds. And you can use it to help the human brain replicate the movements and spaces of a musical performance, to make a listener really feel that they are at a real performance.

This is important, because it's crucial to how a company like Meridian works. Actually, it's fundamental, the central tenet to the brand's method of building really good audio equipment. We're talking about £35,000-for-a-pair-of-speakers worth of good here. At this level, you need to be doing a lot more than making sure the system's got a USB connection. You need to be producing speakers that are so good, you could tell the make of the piano you're hearing, if your listening skills are good enough to be able to do such a thing.

And the point of all of this? How does it make any difference to a Land Rover, or any other car? Because Land Rover, and Jaguar, uses Meridian audio in its cars. Actually, it's done a bit more than that with the Range Rover, by getting Meridian to design the world's first 3D surround-sound system for a car, and psychoacoustics helped to define how it works and what it sounds like.

Meridian has also chosen the very specific locations of some of the 29 speakers you get if you order the Signature Reference system, to use its proper name. Part of the 3D concept is speakers above and behind you, but you don't get any high frequencies from them because, says Meridian's Graham Landick (who runs the division that does the car audio), we don't like loud, high-pitched noise from above and behind us.

We're hard-wired from our past, when we lived in fear of being eaten by predators or having our children plucked off the ground by birds of prey.

Meridian didn't define the concept of psychoacoustics, but it has done lots

> ## "As it turns out, it isn't necessarily harder to design in-car audio than speakers and amps for home use"

of other clever things. In 1974, two smart chaps called Bob Stuart and Allen Boothroyd (an electronics and audio engineer, and an industrial designer) had a go at rethinking an amplifier.

They separated the pre-amp from the rest of the amplifier, made it look like a cylindrical heater, then designed a frankly astonishing control system for the amp: all colour gradients and sliders set in an ultra-matt black casing. It doesn't even look like a piece of home audio, and it definitely doesn't look as though it's 38 years old. You can even find one on display in the New York Museum of Modern Art.

And so it carried on. The world's first audiophile CD player (one that was really good, rather than just a generic consumer product), the world's first digital speaker, the proprietary lossless coding on Blu-ray discs, and an Emmy award.

Unlike so many other manufacturers Meridian also doesn't constantly update the look of its products to create instant obsolescence – the 808 Signature Reference Reference CD player looks exactly the same as it did when it was launched in 1998. It isn't dated, either, because it's such a simple, clean design. And if you want to get the higher specification of the later models, then Meridian can quite

literally slot the new circuitry into your existing machine for you.

Then a couple of years ago Jaguar Land Rover rang up and said: "We need something really good for the Evoque - can you help us out?"

It isn't, as it turns out, necessarily harder to design in-car audio than to design speakers and amps for home use. The thing with cars, as Graham points out, is that they're consistent. You know how big the space you're working with is, you know where the listeners will be sitting, you know what materials surround the space. When people buy audio kit and take it home, they could put it anywhere, surrounded by all sorts of surfaces that will compromise the sound, and then they could go and sit in entirely the wrong place and never hear any of what the designers intended. Not in a car.

But there are issues you will only encounter with in-car audio. And the biggest challenge with making this all work in the Range Rover was getting the 29 speakers to work together perfectly – all of the time and for all occupants of the car. Each listener should be able to hear the same thing (which is the best, clearest image), despite the fact that they're sitting in different places. It's

**FAR LEFT**
Meridian's work
relies much more
on handbuilt
craftsmanship than
it does automated
production processes

**LEFT**
Every component is
painstakingly and
microscopically
checked for defects
and inaccuracies

## CAN ANYBODY HEAR ME...?

Pictured above is the inside of an anechoic chamber
(literal translation: without echo), which is one of the
quietest places on Earth. It's so quiet, in fact, that if
you spent too long in here you'd probably start to go a bit
mad. You become the sound, so your heartbeat is amplified
inside your head, which can become fairly disturbing
after 20 minutes. The dense foam absorbs sound
reflections, deadening noises so they don't exist.

**ABOVE, LEFT: BACK SEAT LISTENERS**
Remote stereo control unit allows passengers to control what they hear (and see) from anywhere in the car

**CENTRE, TOP**
Meridian hadn't worked on any car audio systems before Land Rover came calling, first with a proposal for a high-end system for the Evoque, and now with the latest L405 Range Rover

**CENTRE, BOTTOM**
Headrest-mounted monitors allow rear-seat passengers to enjoy TV and DVDs. The speaker beneath is one of 29 dotted around the Range Rover's cabin

**RIGHT, TOP**
Touchscreen technology helps minimise the clutter of buttons on the dashboard

**RIGHT, MIDDLE**
Locations for some of the speakers, like this one mounted in the door, are obvious; others are a little more obscure

**RIGHT AND FAR RIGHT**
Putting the electronics together for the complex Meridian products is a thoroughly time-consuming task

## "Where do you put a big box without compromising boot space or getting in the way of people's feet?"

the sweet spot, the optimum position to get everything from the sound, to hear the guitarist's fingers slide across the strings on the fretboard, to receive every last shimmer of resonance from the voice, to hear her lips part as she starts to sing.

That's where Meridian's Trifield technology is handy. It creates sweet spots all the time for every listener in the car, so you can provide an ideal image (audio engineer speak for where it sounds as though the performer actually is – the bassist on the left, vocalist in the middle and so on) for every occupant.

Then there's the question of where to put all the speakers. This is the interior of a highly complex vehicle, the priorities for which are that it keep its occupants warm, dry, safe, comfortable, not fall apart – that sort of thing. Finding the optimum place for 29 speakers is never going to be simple.

Of course, there are rather obvious positions for some of them. The door speakers are easy, as is the speaker in the middle of the dash. The above-head-height speakers go in the roof lining.

The problems come with the really big one, the subwoofer: the speaker that creates low bass frequencies. Where, in a car, do you put a big box without compromising boot space or getting in the way of people's

feet? It has to be properly bolted down and it can't go in a door, because there's not enough airspace around it. And anyway, it should ideally be in the middle of the car, so it can be as central as possible in relation to the occupants.

You put it under the floor. It's a bit serendipitous, this, but Graham found a big, empty space in the Range Rover's monocoque between the front and rear seats, large enough to accommodate the subwoofer and leave enough space around it for the air to be pushed about.

Graham, by the way, is one of those people who can listen to a piano and tell you what make it is. He's obsessed with Steinways, especially in full concert trim. His uncle was a piano tuner for EMI and used to tune instruments played by the likes of Liberace, so Graham has, it would be fair to say, quite a lot of experience in this sort of thing. And the piano can be a tricky thing for an audio engineer.

"The piano is one of the hardest instruments to reproduce," he says. "It has so many variables – the type of wood, the strings, the hammers, how much the lid is open, how much each pedal is depressed by. Picking all that up is very difficult – you're asking a speaker to try to cope with all of that information." LR

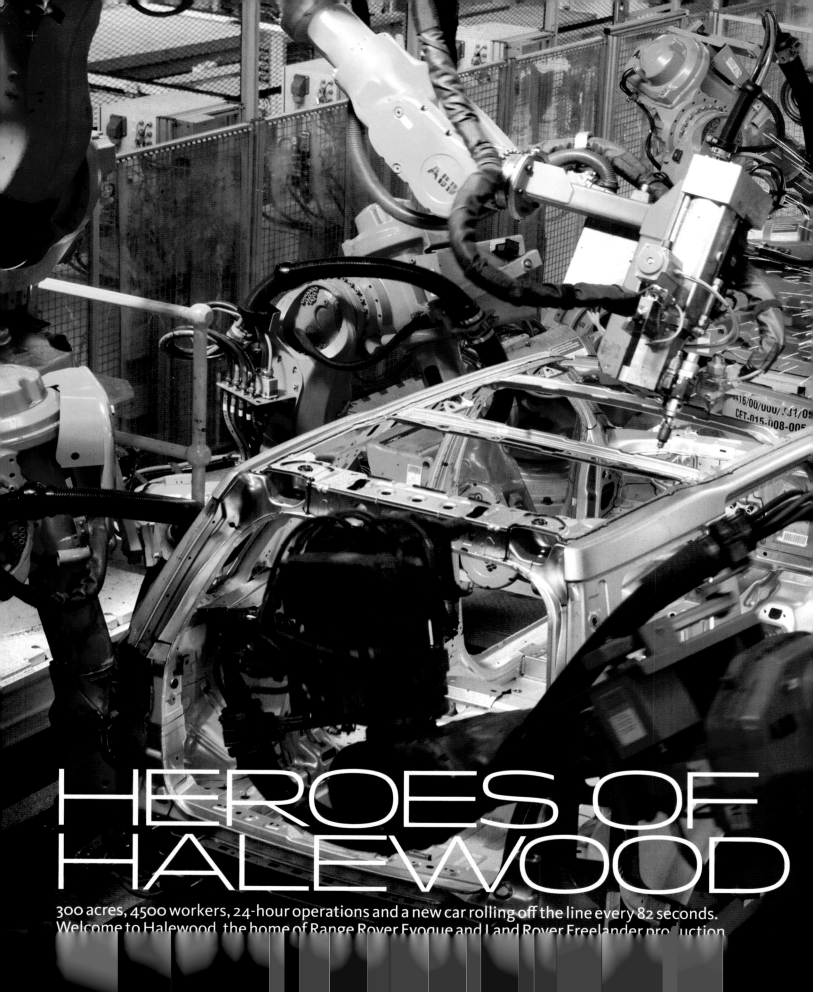

# HEROES OF HALEWOOD

300 acres, 4500 workers, 24-hour operations and a new car rolling off the line every 82 seconds.
Welcome to Halewood, the home of Range Rover Evoque and Land Rover Freelander production

# THE
thought that strikes you as you get your first view of Land Rover's Halewood plant is how big it is. Really, really big. So big that it takes up the whole horizon – you literally cannot see anything but the factory complex, all 300 acres of it, sprawled out in front of you. Pretty it is not, but it is impressive. Even the posters advertising that this is where the Range Rover Evoque and Land Rover Freelander are built are enormous: 40 feet high and 60 feet across, plastered along the side of one of the entrance buildings.

It's something of a fixture on Merseyside, this ever-expanding leviathan, and it's adapted and changed to stay relevant. Ford built it in 1962 to make Anglias, then Escorts, then Jaguar X-Types. It switched to Land Rovers in 2006 with the first Freelander 2, and now builds the Evoque, too. It provides jobs for 4500 workers, operates 24 hours a day, five days a week and the knock-on effect for local suppliers creates even more jobs in a region where unemployment is something of an issue.

The scale of the place is a neat measure of just how incredibly involved and difficult building

## "Nothing else comes close to the sheer space and manpower that's required to build cars"

cars is these days. No other consumer good demands as much sheer manufacturing as a car. The world's largest washing machine factory, in Ohio, employs 3400 people and covers about 60 acres. Even on the very largest scale, nothing else comes close to the sheer space and manpower it takes to build cars.

This is, of course, partly because cars are bigger than washing machines, but also because, if you're pressing the body components, you need a hell of a lot of space. The press shop at Halewood is vast, dominated by 10 lines populated by enormous machines, stamping out the numerous parts that make up a complete bodyshell. Huge coils of steel are unrolled, flattened and then cut into blanks, which are fed into the presses by robots. Next, down comes the press, forming a front chassis leg or a door skin or a roof panel. They're turning out 700 panels an hour – that equates to a total of 26 million parts every year, made out of 125,000 tonnes of steel by 18 million blows of the press onto the die.

Jimmy Rooney keeps an eye on all of this. He's been here for 39 years, since the days of the Escort, and he makes sure that everything coming out of those

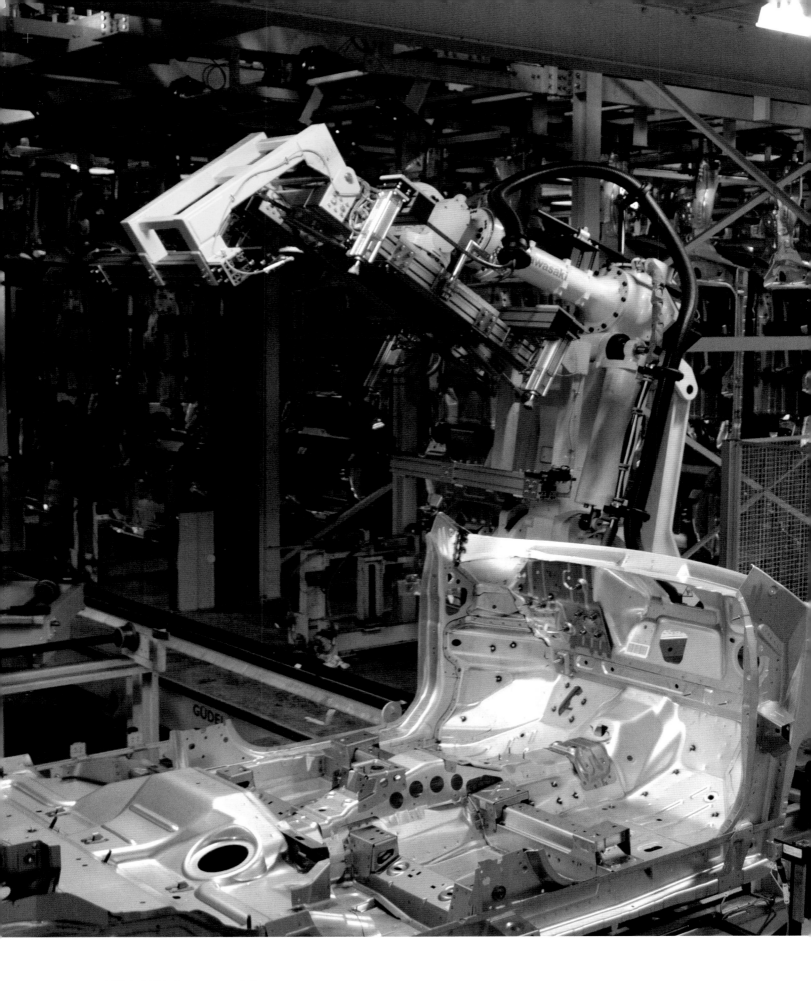

## "Land Rover has trebled the size of the factory's workforce in three years, and it's still expanding"

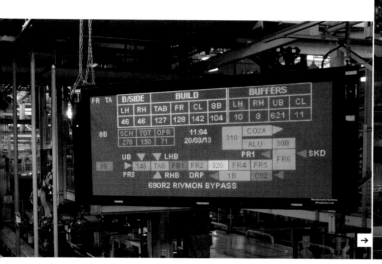

presses is perfect. Jimmy's job is to spot any defects in the panels and then do something about them. He is constantly checking and analysing panels as they come off the line, and if he needs to change anything he has to do it quickly. Because this plant is not only making parts for itself, it's also supplying steel and aluminium panels to Land Rover's Solihull factory for the Range Rover and Range Rover Sport. There are lots of model variants, and a lot of information.

Back when Jimmy started at Halewood, there were 17,500 people working there. Today's figure of 4500 is testament to massively increased automation, but Land Rover has trebled the workforce in three years and it's still expanding. They're adding another line in the press shop to speed up production, which is a bit of a squeeze, because this place is nearly full.

But the press shop, with its high roof and wide walkways, feels positively spacious compared to the body line, where the shells are put together. Every part of this process is carried out by robots, which have transformed not only the way cars are built, but also the whole factory environment and the quality of the cars we drive. Everyone who's been here

for longer than the robots says the same thing – it's a much cleaner, safer, nicer place to work now than it was before. Human beings don't have to get involved with the actual construction of the bodyshells – they're there to keep an eye on it all, to make sure the robots do their job properly.

So it goes something like this. First, the sides and underbodies are welded together separately, on two different lines. The three components (two sides and the floor, with the crash structures) are then joined together and welded up. Finally the roof goes on, followed by the closures – those are the doors, bonnet and tailgate in layman's terms.

The Evoque's rear hatch, which is plastic, gets fitted during the trim stage. It also has aluminium roof panels, which means it disappears off to another line, where robots rivet the pieces in.

Compared to welding steel, riveting aluminium is actually a genuinely quiet and clean process, with no messy sparks or slag to deal with. And it significantly reduces energy consumption compared to welding steel. There's a whole section of the line that's dedicated to removing weld flash from the steel shells

## "Humans don't need to get involved with constructing the bodyshells"

before they're painted. Aluminium-bodied cars don't need this sort of treatment.

You'd never think it, what with all of the terrifying complexity of actually building the cars, but one of the biggest problems the plant had to overcome recently was storage. When it moved to a 24-hour shift to satisfy demand, especially for the Evoque, Land Rover found a problem. It could build enough shells to keep up with that demand, but needed storage.

Traditionally, underbodies are stacked on top of each other, but Halewood is a little short on space, and there was nowhere to cram in the 700-odd underbodies that have to be kept in reserve for weekend production. So they built the Kipper Rack. Underbodies are hung vertically, in long rows, like kippers in a smoker, which is a much more efficient use of space. The rack will typically be empty on a Friday evening, when production stops, then it refills over the weekend, ready for production to restart on Monday morning.

And this is where it gets really complicated. Up until now, shells have been built to order – in other words, the factory knows how many right-hand-drive, three-door Evoques with panoramic roofs are

required. But it's at this point the cars start to gain more of an individual identity. They're painted, which involves being dipped in electro-phosphate to act as a corrosion preventative, and then baked in an oven. A coat of primer is applied, then they go back in the oven, then the base colour is put on, followed by clearcoat.

As the car comes out of the paint shop, it's assigned a specification in the form of a piece of paper stuck to the carrier that the car is hung on. There are 380,000 potential configurations that could pass through this factory. The destination for each vehicle is on the spec sheet, and watching them come down the line you can see that every one is going off somewhere different. Spain. Algeria. China. Mexico. France. Russia.

The logistics involved are staggering. The moment the car's specification is assigned, it's relayed to Land Rover's suppliers – the companies that provide parts like the front bumpers, seats and carpets. They're all based quite close to the factory, so parts arrive quickly and are stacked behind the trim shop.

The place is insanely busy with forklifts. There are hundreds of them, whirling and spinning their way through the narrow roadways, loaded with boxes and

Zone 23, St 60

ZONE 23 STN 060 CPU 1
CLOSURE FIT PROCESS
CV-110-060

"The assembly workers move with fluidity and ease, but there's very little room for error"

## ALUMINIUM: LIGHT AND STRONG

These days, aluminium cars are more mainstream, but Land Rover's been using it for longer than most. Since 1947, in fact. Rover used it originally because it was easier to get hold of than steel, which was rationed, rather than for environmental reasons.

The original Range Rover always used aluminium body panels, and today's Defender still uses aluminium panels. It's a very light and strong material that doesn't corrode as dramatically as steel.

Today, Land Rover uses aluminium in a much more advanced way, spending £370m on the production line at Solihull. That means it's now the world's biggest aluminium car plant.

The presses produce an entire Range Rover side panel, the world's largest single automtive pressing, in one piece, so there are fewer joins, which makes the car stiffer than one with welds. The rest of the Range Rover's 403 panels and parts are joined together with a total of 3722 rivets.

Land Rover also claims the aluminium shop uses 75 per cent less power than a steel line, and there's also the advantage of being able to recycle and sell off the waste. That brings in an extra £1.7m every year - and some of it could find its way back into a Range Rover, as 50 per cent of the raw material used is recycled.

**LEFT**
In the paint shop, the cars are first dipped in electro-phosphate, which prevents corrosion. They're then baked in an oven, before a coat of primer is applied. There's a second visit to the oven, then the base colour is put on, followed by clearcoat

crates of parts, or towing trailers carrying complete front-end assemblies. They start at the warehouse where the parts are picked and then head for the lines. It's exceptionally busy, and just getting all the right parts to the right locations in the factory is, in itself, a feat of organisation .

And while the half-finished Evoques and Freelanders look as if they're trundling down the production line at a fairly sedate speed, and the workers fitting the wiring harnesses, seats and carpets move with fluidity and ease, there's very little room for error. They work at the pace of the line, and each task has an allocated time during which it must be completed. Markings painted on the floor designate where each task has to end, although if the car is higher-spec and needs more equipment installed, there is some leeway to run over a little.

The trim shop is almost entirely operated by humans. It's the least automated area of the factory, as it would be impossible to programme a robot to keep track of the constant variations. Plus, some of the more constricted areas of the car just can't be reached by machines. A lot of what's done here requires

BELOW
Engine and gearbox
are assembled on a
separate production
line, before a
machine called
the Stuffer (left)
lowers the body on to
drivetrain in just
20 seconds. At the
moment, Halewood
produces five
Evoques for every
two Freelanders,
and operates a
24-hour shift
pattern (right)

what Steve Wilson, Halewood's final assembly production manager, describes as 'finessing'. Or, in other words, adjusting things by hand a little to make them absolutely perfect.

However, there isn't much chance of error. Take how the badges are attached to the cars, for example. There are an awful lot of different badges, so the rack next to the line containing them has a light under each compartment. When the car arrives, a transponder with the specification programmed into it tells the rack which badge is needed. The correct light then illuminates, so the fitter knows which one to pick.

From here on, the cars are built up in pretty much the order you might expect. With the wiring installed, the dash is fitted (all one piece, with the wheel removed for the Evoque, as the dash won't go in through the door aperture with the wheel on), followed by the fuel tank, brake lines, bumpers and windows.

The engine and gearbox are united on another line, and they get fitted to a jig, which also takes the front and rear subframes with the suspension, propshaft and brakes. This entire assembly is then rolled

## "Who says we don't make anything in Great Britain anymore?"

under the shell, lifted up and bolted in – it only takes about 20 seconds to fit from start to finish. Factory workers call the machine that joins the shell to the drivetrain the Stuffer.

And that – aside from the seats, wheels and fluids – is that. A complete vehicle rolls off the production line at Halewood every 82 seconds – currently five Evoques to every two Freelanders. They're programmed, put through a leak test and then driven outside to be subjected to all sorts of different surfaces (cobbles, rumble strips, rough paving), which should detect rattles or loose parts that need to be rectified.

Spend a morning watching this process, from a coil of steel to a complete Evoque, and you come away somewhat blinded by the scale and complexity of it all. And yet it never seems impersonal or dehumanised, because despite all the robots and presses and automation there's still a huge human involvement in making cars. People are everywhere at Halewood, carrying out some of the most crucial and delicate operations involved in taking that steel and converting it into a new car. So who says we don't make anything inGreat Britain anymore? LR

RIGHT
A complete new car
rolls off Halewood's
production line
every 82 seconds.
It's then driven over
a variety of harsh
road surfaces and
leak-tested to
spot any defects
that might have
to be rectified

# THE PEOPLE

**Land Rover's as much about the people who work there as it is the vehicles they produce, and the people who use the vehicles in difficult conditions**

# THE ARCHITECT

As Land Rover's Design Director, he's the man who decides how its vehicles will look. But Gerry McGovern is obsessed with architecture. So Steve Fowler asks how he ended up designing cars. And what's with the collection of 150 chairs?

# FILE

under 'tough gig': reinventing an iconic brand by transforming a well loved and historic line-up, while attracting a whole new breed of luxury car buyers with a range of all-new models that must all be true to the company's DNA.

That's the challenge Gerry McGovern took on when he rejoined Land Rover in 2004, initially as director of advanced design, before he became design director in 2006. Since then, McGovern has added chief creative officer to his business card, so he's now responsible for the look of pretty much everything you see that's associated with the Land Rover brand, from advertising to showroom furniture.

This is McGovern's second stint with Land Rover. In the nineties, while he was working for Rover, he was the lead designer on the original award-winning Land Rover Freelander. He also has the MGF sports car to his name. Today, he describes those two cars as "a bit primitive". I think he's being a bit harsh, to be honest.

Meeting McGovern is always something I look forward to – when he talks, he avoids much of the designerese that his rivals often spout, using as much care and thought about the words he chooses as the lines he draws. He's passionate about all aspects of design, not just cars, and that's what I'm in New York to talk to him about.

He glides into the Four Seasons Restaurant in New York, a couple of days after the headline-grabbing launch of the Range Rover Sport. He looks every inch the perfect English gent: piercing blue eyes, well cut hair and dressed in the best Savile Row has to offer. He's a walking advert for the best of British... almost. His shoes are Italian. Handmade, of course.

The new Range Rover Sport arrived in New York with another British gent behind the wheel – James Bond himself, Daniel Craig. Craig is often thought of as a paragon of British style, yet I debate with McGovern whether Craig's particular choice of attire will still look good when we all look back at the pictures in a few year's time. "Clothes are a very personal thing" says McGovern. I counter by claiming that Craig's slim-fitting suit is a little too 'now' and might date slightly. "Daniel Craig would look good in anything" says McGovern.

The Four Seasons restaurant was McGovern's choice for lunch – it's one of his favourite haunts in New York, as it sits in one of his favourite buildings – the Seagram Tower on Park Avenue.

This 1950s skyscraper highlights McGovern's incredible passion for architecture – he talks with great authority and detail on the subject, telling the story of Mies van der Rohe, who was responsible for the exterior, and Philip Johnson, who designed the interior that includes the stunning restaurant we're sitting in. "When the building opened in 1958, it was the first modernist skyscraper in New York. Others were art deco inspired, yet this took a new, clean and sheer approach," explains McGovern.

"Every line has a consequence and the way Mies took the inside to the outside with such beauty and detail is outstanding: the straight lines of the steel I-beams, the huge bronzed glass panels, the brass, the marble."

"When the building first opened, people were worried about sitting so close to the glass right at the edge of the building. They actually employed a big guy to run straight at the glass to prove that it was strong enough."

The Four Seasons restaurant is luxurious yet business-like, with enormous veneers adorning the walls and original, if re-trimmed, Brno chairs that were designed by Mies himself.

"This was the first restaurant in New York to use seasonal ingredients," says McGovern, "Which is how it came to be called the Four Seasons. And this is where President John F Kennedy dined with Marilyn Monroe on the evening in which she sang her famous 'happy birthday' tribute to him."

As if to prove the point about the history and power within the walls of the Four Seasons, none other than former US secretary of state Henry Kissinger is sitting on an adjacent table.

**MCGOVERN CITES** Palm Springs in California as another of his favourite places – home to the rich, famous and retired, and with a plethora of modernist homes. Frank Sinatra's house, designed by E Stewart Williams, mixes clean, elegant, straight edges with a piano shaped swimming pool, while the iconic John Lautner designed Elrod house, used in the Bond movie Diamonds are Forever, together with Neutra's Kaufman House, which epitomises the inside outside look, are some of McGovern's favourites.

McGovern reels off a list of his other favourite architects including Eero Saarinen and Pierre Koenig – all famous for their use of simple lines and curves, which have inspired McGovern's own self-penned modernist home set into the side of a hill in deepest Warwickshire.

So why is he designing cars and not buildings? "Architecture represented static objects and cars moving objects. Back then the latter had more pull."

McGovern was born in Coventry to Irish parents, neither of whom could drive a car. His early car memories were courtesy of friends and family members' cars and he sheepishly recalls an early admiration for the Vauxhall Cresta – not exactly known as a design classic.

"From an early age I was aesthetically aware," he recalls, "And my mother was quite artistic – I was a kid in the 60s when there was a decent level of modernism around and I remember my mother's fascination with Robin and Lucienne Day wallpaper."

McGovern's career was shaped by one particular car designer he met, thanks to his art teacher: "I started getting heavily into art when I was 15 or 16. I wanted to be an artist, but soon realised that you don't really make any money as an artist until you're dead! So I started thinking of car design as an option – not many people did back then. Automotive design wasn't as high profile as it is today, so in some respects it was a more difficult career path.

"My art teacher's brother-in-law introduced me to the HR manager of Chrysler in the UK, who arranged for me to meet someone in the design team.

**LEFT AND FAR LEFT**
Gerry McGovern in front of (and inside) the Seagram building in Manhattan. The 1958 skyscraper, designed by Mies van de Rohe, was one of the first Modernist buildings in the city, and one of McGovern's favourite buildings

**FAR LEFT**
Inside McGovern's own Modernist creation, his house in Warwickshire. Hanging on the wall above the table are two silkscreens by British artist Patrick Heron

## His favourite architects are all famous for their use of simple lines and curves, which have inspired his own self-penned home

That person couldn't make it, so Roy Axe, Chrysler's design boss at the time, stepped in."

The two obviously clicked, because on finishing his industrial design course in Coventry, he went on to study automotive design at the Royal College of Art, before joining the Chrysler design team. After stints with Chrysler in the US, Axe took him with him to Rover, where he stayed until Ford headhunted him in 1999, asking him to head up the Lincoln/Mercury design team back in the US. Finally, in 2004 he headed back to Land Rover.

It took a while for a real McGovern Land Rover to surface – the 2008 LRX concept which, pretty much unchanged, became the Range Rover Evoque. That was followed by the DC100 concept, last year's all-new Range Rover and now the Range Rover Sport.

All have been heavily influenced by McGovern's modernist beliefs that every line has to have a purpose and that modernism is about reduction: "That's why I'm keen to reduce clutter – especially inside our cars," he says.

I point out that many of the design inspirations he talks about aren't exactly modern – mid-age as he describes them himself – yet he's designing the most modern of luxury items. "One of the reasons I resonate with mid-century modern is because of its proven longevity. What those guys created in that period still looks as modern today and is still just as relevant.

"I love contemporary modern too, especially furniture from B&B Italia. For me, it's a mix of classic modernism, mid-century modern and contemporary modern and that's been my approach to the way I've organised the interior of my home. Modernism is quite often mistaken for minimalism; I'm certainly not an advocate of minimalism, I'm actually quite eclectic. The thing that ties them all together for me is the design approach."

**AS WELL AS ARCHITECTURE,** McGovern has a big passion for furniture and especially chairs. That's not all that surprising really, as he explains, "Lots of architects do furniture to go inside the buildings they create – Mies for example, with the chairs in the Four Seasons restaurant in the Seagram building." His own furniture collection is comprehensive and represents his values of creativity. He pulls out his iPhone to show me photos of his Eames chair, "It dates from 1948 and is still one of the most comfortable chairs in the world – you'll be asleep within five minutes of sitting in it."

The latest addition to his collection is an Eero Aarnio ball chair that hangs from the ceiling by a chain, designed in the 1960s, while he also has the Tulip collection designed by Eero Saarinen for Knoll. "Saarinen's philosophy was also to get rid of clutter. His ambition when designing the Tulip Collection was to remove what he described as the slum of legs. Think about it – traditionally a chair would have had four legs, a table four legs; multiply the chairs by four and you have 20 legs. He reduced that number to five, by creating a single pedestal on each piece."

There are also egg chairs and swan chairs in McGovern's homes, the latter having what all the best design should have in varied measure, according to McGovern: a sense of fun.

It's London design that really resonates. "London presents luxury in a more reserved way" he says. "And luxury can be about being discreet"

He loves to collect art too, with pictures of works he owns from the likes of Patrick Heron, Josef Albers and Patrick Caulfield on his iPhone. So what about the gadgets? McGovern clearly makes good use of his iPhone.

"I know [Apple designer] Sir Johnny Ive; we're currently working on a small design project. We share similar views on design philosophy and I have a great deal of respect for what he's achieved at Apple. He's worked tirelessly to put design at the core of their business and it shows in everything they do. I have several Apple products – iMac, MacBook Pro, iPads and of course the iPhone. I use them for both business and pleasure. The iPhone can be a bit touch sensitive, but that's more me than it. I wouldn't be without it. But gadgetry in general can do my head in on occasions."

"We have to remember though that products, no matter how desirable from a design perspective, need to do what they're meant to do. That's a given."

That applies to McGovern's watches, too. His choice for our meeting in New York is a stunning rose gold Rolex. An unusual choice for a man who likes simple lines, I suggest? "Yes, but it's a classic and I feel the fussiness is appropriate on such a luxury item. Jewel-like quality for me warrants more detail, don't you think?"

Out comes the iPhone again, with pictures of a few carefully selected watches: the iconic Nautilus, designed by Gerald Genta in the 1970s and a Submariner with a green chromium bezel and face, which McGovern describes as very Land Rover. "For me watches represent a level of precision and craftsmanship that I aspire to achieve in our vehicles."

The US, especially Palm Springs and New York, may well inspire McGovern in his work, but it's London design that really resonates with him from a cultural perspective. And that's where we head next, meeting at Henry Poole, his tailor of choice.

"London presents luxury in a more reserved way," he says, "And true luxury can be about being discreet."

Henry Poole was established in 1806, and McGovern ranks as one of its most discerning customers today, with several Henry Poole suits in his collection. "I've done all the fashion brands over time and while I like them they never fit me properly and can't compare with a bespoke suit. I've also tried other tailors in Savile Row, too, but this is where I'm most comfortable," he says. "This is one of my passions, it's a hobby and I find it very therapeutic."

Again McGovern makes comparisons with automotive world. "Craftsmanship is the obvious one, but it goes much further than that and it's not just about the end product. The way Poole nurture a long-term relationship with the customers that is often collaborative is a very interesting one. Most pertinent for me is the fact that the majority of Henry Poole's customers are our customers too."

It's the personal relationship that's important to McGovern and I'm introduced to Alex Cooke, managing director of Henry Poole and the man who still cuts McGovern's suits. "Gerry's suits are based upon what's termed the classic West End cut, a shape that absolutely epitomises Savile Row tailoring," Cooke tells me. "We talk about shape and shoulder line – there's a

**LEFT**
Cufflinks, ties and material line stacked up at Savile Row tailor Henry Poole, where McGovern has his suits made

**ABOVE**
McGovern explains his love for bespoke tailoring; he describes the process as therapeutic

**TOP**
Henry Poole's managing director Alex Cooke talks through material choices and styles

little bit of chest and extra tapering at the waist. We work on the choice of fabrics and the cut together."

Cooke has been at Henry Poole's for 18 years, after taking a degree in women's wear: "You learn more about cutting," he explains.

A typical Henry Poole suit is a considerable investment, but as Cooke says: "It'll last years and years – about ten times as long as an off-the-peg suit. Many of our customers will buy a couple of suits a year and they're mostly bankers, lawyers, a few architects, doctors from LA. We're not really celebrity tailors."

But for the computers holding details of customers' suits that have replaced the huge ledgers that still sit on the shelves, Poole's is refreshingly tech-free. No more so than in the workshops downstairs, where we meet Paul, 54 years a tailor and the man who makes many of McGovern's jackets. On his work board are the simple tools of his artistry as well as a huge, ancient-looking iron. Like McGovern, Paul has worked with James Bond, as he's created suit jackets for the likes of Sean Connery and Roger Moore.

"I like the Britishness of these suits," says McGovern. "Land Rover is a British brand and I suppose people expect me to look British. I had a particular suit made for the Range Rover launch in LA – a specially-made pin-stripe that was very British."

McGovern sums up: "Tailoring is similar in some respects to car design, it's not all subjective. It's an art – it's all about balance, proportion and shape as well as appropriate detailing."

### WHILE POOLE'S PROVIDES McGovern's suits,
Sean O'Flynn is his shirt maker, working out of Sackville Street, which is just around the corner from Savile Row.

"Gerry's quite experimental with colour and fabric," says O'Flynn. "He likes to try out different things and together we work out what's feasible. We started out quite classical with white, then moved on to colours with contrasting collars and cuffs."

"The desire for people to personalise, whether it be clothing or a vehicle, is gaining greater relevance than ever before. So as we develop our vehicles, this desire must be given greater consideration" says McGovern.

"The nicest thing is that Sean's shirts get better with age, and of course the ability to personalise them is endless. I have two types of shirts: a dress shirt that I wear with a tie that has a double cuff. Then there's what we term the casual shirt, always worn opened necked although it is dual purpose.

"It can be quite dressy when worn with a jacket, it has a deep collar so it sits perfectly within the jacket lapels and it has a single cuff, buttons not cufflinks, that I quite often wear open. It can also be worn without a jacket over jeans as these shirts are deliberately cut not too long in the body."

"Clothes have to be appropriate," he adds. "There's an element of judgment that has to be applied. As a creative person, I can get away with being more flamboyant, but then I have to remember that I'm representing the company at a senior level and I'm an ambassador for the brand."

**ABOVE**
Art is as much of a passion as clothes - McGovern's preference is for clean, simple lines and the sharpness of printing

**BELOW**
McGovern explains his ideas of displaying art. "It's not just about the picture, it's got to work in a particular space"

**RIGHT**
The new Range Rover parked on Savile Row, where some of the ideas that informed its interior and exterior design originated

## McGovern plans his home meticulously, siting appropriate furniture, rugs or artefacts alongside his art

We've already touched on McGovern's love of art and our final stop is around the corner in Cork Street and the Alan Cristea Gallery, where Alan Cristea himself is outside waiting for us. McGovern is a frequent visitor here, whether to browse, buy or just chat – and Cristea is more than happy to do any one of them.

We're led downstairs into a private viewing room where McGovern shows me Patrick Caulfield's Spider Plant, which he has hanging in his house. "I've got that next to a window, and the picture mirrors the landscape outside. It's not just about the picture, it's got to work in a particular space and is about how the whole room relates to the art or vice versa," he explains.

Cristea has known McGovern for about 12 years and the two clearly enjoy discussing some of the artists Cristea represents. "Everything Gerry buys has clean, simple lines," Cristea tells me.

"For me it's about economy of line, shape and colour," says McGovern. "I really like printing because of the sharpness of line you get, especially when printing on silkscreen. Ultimately it has to resonate with me on an emotional level. That's the differentiator between ordinary and special."

Cristea shows me some examples of Ian Davenport's poured lines, and we discuss McGovern's Caulfield pictures: "Caulfield often depicted scenes after human beings have left and often with a huge sense of irony. He was one of the first so-called 'pop artists' – a generation of English artists who went to college together, including the likes of David Hockney."

McGovern plans his home meticulously, sitting appropriate furniture, rugs or artefacts alongside his art, even going so far as repainting one wall a dark grey to make a black-on-white Caulfield print stand out even more effectively on the wall.

"With art, you either buy to collect or you buy to enjoy," says McGovern. "I do the latter."

Leaning against the wall of the viewing room is a striking Michael Craig-Martin print McGovern is considering purchasing, from the Seven Deadly Sins collection. This particular one is called Pride, and it's a mix of solid pink, purple and violet.

While it's strong in colour, I point out that it doesn't exactly fit in with McGovern's philosophy of clean, simple lines.

"Yes, there's a lot going on," concedes McGovern, "But it's very well considered and has such a sense of optimism, I don't consider pride a sin. I like what it says and I love its graphic and balance."

After a thoughtful pause, he continues: "I never would have considered this picture before Vanessa came along."

With that he reaches again for his iPhone and shows me what is clearly of his favourite and most important picture: one of him sitting with his three-year old daughter at the dinner table.

"She's already becoming aesthetically aware – even of her food, which she won't eat if not presented in a visually pleasing way. And after all," says the proud father, "they're what we do it all for." LR

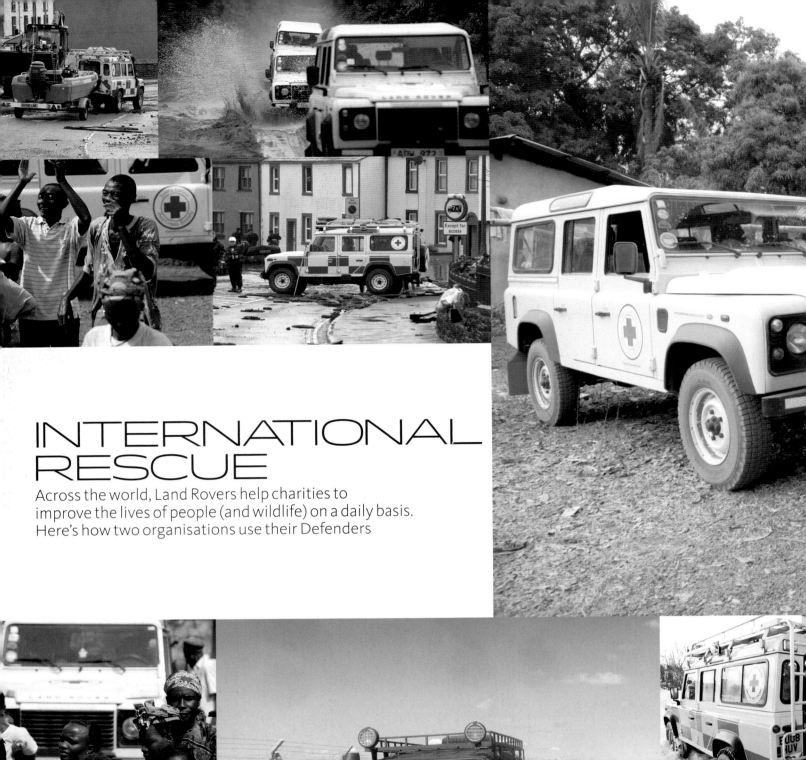

# INTERNATIONAL RESCUE

Across the world, Land Rovers help charities to improve the lives of people (and wildlife) on a daily basis. Here's how two organisations use their Defenders

When it comes to helping people, there are few organisations that have such a long history as the Red Cross Red Crescent. And its relationship with Land Rover has been going since 1954, when the British Red Cross 107-inch Series I was delivered for use as a mobile dispensary in Dubai. The Red Cross Red Crescent has used Land Rovers across the world for its humanitarian work, and in 2007 it formed an official partnership with Land Rover. That was the year Land Rover turned 60, and the firm donated 60 vehicles to the Movement.

That partnership has helped the Red Cross in countries such as Sierra Leone, where the organisation has been working to reunite communities ripped apart by the long civil war – especially children. The Land Rovers enable the Red Cross Red Crescent to get to the remote villages that were often forgotten about in the aftermath of the war, and to begin the rehabilitation of the victims of the conflict. Red Cross Red Crescent drivers have also been trained by Land Rover in off-road driving techniques, crucial to their work in places without roads.

Land Rover has also helped the Red Cross in Liberia, with donations of Defenders to tackle the roads there, which were badly damaged during the civil war and become extremely hard work during the rainy season. The Land Rovers make it possible to get around.

But it's not only countries overseas that need the help of the Red Cross Red Crescent. Half of the donated vehicles stayed in the UK and over the last three winters the Red Cross has been using Land Rovers to reach people in need trapped in heavy snow. The vehicles have been assisting the emergency services, getting people to hospital, delivering medical supplies and getting food to people trapped in their houses. Land Rover also loans Defenders to the Red Cross in the UK if it needs more vehicles in a hurry.

Since 2007, Land Rover has provided support to the Red Cross Red Crescent worth £6.4m, which has benefitted 680,000 people across the planet. ᒪᑌ

**TOP**
The Red Cross at work in the UK, using the Defender to reach people trapped by heavy snowfall

**ABOVE**
Land Rover loans extra vehicles to the Red Cross in the UK for when bad weather strikes, as it did here in Scotland

**MIDDLE**
A Defender in a village in Sierra Leone, where the Red Cross has been working to restore communities damaged by war

**RIGHT**
Land Rovers have helped Red Cross staff help communities become more self-sufficient

The relationship between the Red Cross and Land Rover has been going since 1954

## ALL CREATURES GREAT AND SMALL

Land Rover doesn't just help people. Its vehicles have been used by the wildlife charity Born Free Foundation since it began in 1984, and the charity's founders had been driving them for years before that.

Born Free and Land Rover established an official partnership in 2002, and since then the charity has had Land Rovers working across Africa - Zimbabwe, South Africa, Ethiopia and Kenya - as well as Sri Lanka and the UK.

The vehicles are working on projects such as the Ethopian Wolf Conservation Programme, monitoring wolf populations in the Arsi Mountains and vaccinating the wolves against rabies. In Sri Lanka, a Defender is being used to rescue

orphan elephants and in Kenya, Born Free Land Rovers are used for anti-poaching patrols and to rescue animals caught in traps. They also provide transport so staff can get to villages and schools to help educate people about wildlife conservation.

Born Free has also started to protect villagers' livestock from lion attack by building predator-proof enclosures. These reinforced 'bomas' have proved to be a successful method of reducing the number of big cats killed in retaliation for taking livestock, and the Land Rovers enable the foundation to reach the villages.

"Land Rover's support gives us the backing we need to carry out frontline conservation on a daily basis," says Born Free's Will Travers.

# COMPANY MAN

Roger Crathorne has worked on almost every Land Rover project
for the past 50 years – but he remains focused on the future

**THE MORE YOU** talk to Roger Crathorne, the more you struggle to believe what he's saying. He was closely involved with the development engineering on the first Range Rover, effectively defining what it would become. In the seventies, he ran a project looking at how to replace the Land Rover – a vehicle that had changed the world for decades. He's worked at the company since 1963, and successfully bridged the gap between the disparate worlds of engineering and marketing. He's been involved with just about every car the company has launched in the past 50 years. He was even born in Lode Lane, where Land Rover has its factory, in 1947 – the same year the Land Rover was conceived. So it's difficult to comprehend how close he is to the brand, and what he's done.

When Roger joined Rover as a service apprentice, Land Rover made one model. Now there are six, and a move upmarket has changed the company hugely. Remember, the Range Rover was not launched as a luxury SUV, but as a more comfortable alternative to the Land Rover – although Roger had a hand in that, too. The story goes that, in order to insulate a noisy gearbox, he covered the transmission tunnel in his own Range Rover in carpet. Then he had a set of carpets fitted, and it improved the interior no end – the model's journey to the position it occupies today had begun.

But it's Roger's adaptability that's kept him relevant to this day. Today, he's Land Rover's technical PR manager. Talk to him about

In typical Land Rover style, Crathorne's work has taken him to some interesting places. Here, he's in France, in a tuxedo (of course) filming for French TV

"Roger looks forward – to how the industry will develop and what Land Rover's place in it will be"

the brand, and he's looking forward all the time – to how the car industry will develop and what Land Rover's place in it will be.

"Downsizing isn't always the way forward," he says. "Customers still want big cars, and they keep speccing them up with kit." So Land Rover's challenge is to cut weight and increase efficiency. Then there's the perennial and vexatious question of replacing the Defender. "We have to think outside of the box for Defender," he says. "It needs to be equally capable of cruising along a Californian beach and shunting a farm gate open in Wales."

So what about the Land Rover that should have been – the car Roger would like to have built, but couldn't? "The 100-inch Station Wagon should have made it through," he says. This was effectively a Land Rover crew-cab, years before the crew-cab became the layout of choice for working pick-ups. It was ahead of its time, and good enough to displace the short-wheelbase Land Rover in the company's product plans for a while. But a lack of funding to develop the new body meant the project was shelved.

And despite the successes he's been involved with through the years, Roger doesn't see the Land Rover of the past as some kind of idealistic utopia. "Now we have a management team that will finance the next set of ideas," he explains. "The sixties was definitely a golden period for Land Rover, but we couldn't afford to develop all the ideas we came up with back then. Now, we can." LR

**LEFT**
Today, Crathorne works as Land Rover's technical PR manager, using his experience to help communicate one of the British motor industry's greatest success stories

# LAND ROVER

# THE VEHICLES

From testing the new Range Rover Sport in the Arctic Circle to how the Evoque was taken from concept car to finished product – the cars that make Land Rover what it is today

# SURVIVAL OF THE FITTEST

Tom Phillips joins the engineers testing the all-new Range Rover Sport – which offers sports car dynamics and SUV stamina – amidst the frozen lakes and punishing off-road terrain of Arjeplog, in the far north of Sweden

Polcirkeln
Napapiiri
Arctic Circle
Cercle Polaire
Polarkreis

Norrbottens län

For eight months of the year, precisely nothing happens in the town of Arjeplog in northern Sweden. But come December, all of that changes. The town's population of around 3,000 more than doubles, as up to 4,000 test engineers from the world's biggest car makers and their suppliers descend on this remote location. For the four months of winter, from early December to late March, they flock here to take advantage of temperatures that regularly plummet to minus 20 degrees Celsius and below. That allows icy test tracks to be cut into the frozen surface of the lakes around the town, creating the perfect environment for pushing prototype cars to breaking point.

We've come to Arjeplog for a ride in the all-new Range Rover Sport. It's so new that the car we're sampling is a pre-production development model, wearing the sort of camouflage usually reserved for the Swedish army. We'll be taking to the frozen lakes as vehicle engineering manager Craig Carter and off-road capability group leader Jason Walters complete the sign-off process for the new Sport's stability control and Terrain Response 2 systems.

But we'll also be hitting public roads to go even further north, taking the car into the Arctic Circle. We'll be accompanied by the current and previous generations of the regular Range Rover, so we can switch between the three cars to get a better impression of how the new Sport feels compared to the old and new flagship models.

Despite the disguise, you can tell that the new Sport has a wide, stocky stance that makes the latest Range Rover seem big and tall, and the old Sport seem a little square and dated. This is helped by the fact that the new Sport's wheelbase has been increased over the previous model's, giving extra space inside for up to seven seats.

Ground clearance is higher than the old car's, yet the roofline is lower. However, when you swing open the passenger door, step over the chunky side sill and get behind the wheel, you'll find the latest Sport has retained the raised, commanding driving position that's become a distinctive Range Rover trademark over the years.

The company's engineers have worked hard to ensure that the new Sport is more clearly differentiated from the luxurious regular Range Rover this time. In fact, both engineers tell us that this has been the most difficult, yet ultimately the most satisfying, aspect of the car's development. Craig explains: "We found the sweet spot between making it handle really well at the Nürburgring, where the car can lap at around the [hot-hatch-rivalling] eight minutes and 40 seconds mark, and being in a completely different league off-road." He adds: "We can only benchmark the new Sport against our other models off-road, as rivals like the BMW X5 and Porsche Cayenne just can't handle the type of routes we do."

Jason adds that in a planned five-day off-road endurance test, both the X5 and Cayenne lasted for four hours before they had to be loaded onto a transporter and sent back to their respective manufacturers, as they're just not built for the type of off-road punishment that some Range Rover Sport buyers dole out.

The previous Sport was based on the underpinnings of the current Land Rover Discovery, albeit with a different wheelbase, but the new car's advanced glued and riveted aluminium architecture is similar to the latest Range Rover's. Despite this, the models only share 25 per cent of their parts – the major cost savings come instead from the ability to build both cars on the same production line. The lighter platform also helps to slice around 420kg from this V6 diesel-engined version of the Sport.

It's immediately obvious that this car has been designed to feel quite different to the regular Range Rover – even before you drive off. The A-pillars slope back at a sharper angle than the larger car's, and while they share the top of their dashboard, the lower part of the Sport's dash is much less upright, as if the whole Range Rover dash and centre console has been rotated away from the driver. The Sport's centre console is higher than the Range Rover's, and the steering wheel has a 15mm smaller diameter for a sportier feel. This gives you the impression of being cocooned in the car.

The design of the dashboard is considerably less cluttered than that of the previous model of Range Rover Sport. Most of the buttons are gone, with their functions now incorporated into a central touchscreen monitor. The controls that remain have all been transferred to the steering wheel or the centre console. This includes the dials for the climate control and heated seats – both essential companions for driving in the northern Swedish winter.

Instead of the rotary gear selector, the Sport has a proper aluminium gearknob for the automatic transmission. This can be slid to the left for manual shifts, or the driver can use steering-wheel-mounted paddles to flick up and down through the car's

VX12 OCP

"The engineers have worked hard to ensure this new Sport is more clearly differentiated from the Range Rover"

**LEFT**
Sport's sat-nav screen doesn't lie - engineers test prototype and pre-production cars on tracks carved into the frozen surface of Swedish lakes. Manufacturer testing activity supports a mini-industry in the small town of Arjeplog each winter, with full workshop and storage facilities for the engineers and cars

**ABOVE**
Land Rover set its engineers ambitious targets for the new Sport. It had to be capable of lapping the Nürburgring as fast as a hot hatch, yet still leave rivals like the BMW X5 and Porsche Cayenne behind on rougher terrain. The harsh environment of northern Sweden in winter is ideal for proving its off-road capabilities

"You feel the Terrain Response 2 system metering out the power to whichever wheel has the most grip, as well as the effect of Hill Descent Control"

Breathtaking Swedish scenery provides the backdrop for a punishing testing regime. Land Rover has replicated its toughest off-road testing course in the snow just outside Arjeplog, giving the new Sport ample opportunity to flex its formidable all-terrain muscle

"Land Rover's engineer demonstrates the Dynamic mode with spectacular slides across the frozen lake surface"

eight gears. The Sport's Terrain Response 2 system includes all the familiar off-road modes, plus a Dynamic mode that reduces the intervention of the stability control system and increases the responsiveness of the gearbox, throttle and steering. Jason demonstrated the effect of this setting with spectacular slides across the ice, and also showed how it turns the edges of the TFT dials red and displays a large, pool-ball-style graphic of which gear you're in between the rev counter and speedo.

Sliding around on the frozen surface of the lake is as fun as it is informative, but we're keen to hit some public roads to get a better idea of how the new car feels. Before we head to the Arctic Circle, however, we divert to Land Rover's nearby off-road track. This was designed to be a snowier, slipperier version of the toughest route at the company's Eastnor Castle testing centre back in the UK. As the terrain gets progressively rougher, Jason tells us that the new Sport has been designed to offer "effortless composure off-road."

It's impossible to verify that claim without driving the car, but the Sport has no trouble scaling a very slippery slope that's near-impossible to walk up. And it seems tuning of the ARC (adjustable roll control) anti-roll bars has given this car smoother side-to-side movement than the Range Rover. The refinement, even when tackling some pretty rough ground, is very impressive. You can feel the Terrain Response 2 system metering out the power to whichever wheel has the most grip, as well as the effect of the Hill Descent Control, but the interventions are subtler and quieter than before. So although you can go further off-road in a Sport than ever before, the upgraded electronics maintain the calm ambience of the Sport's plush interior almost as well as its bigger brother.

Leaving the Land Rover off-road test track, we head northwest out of town. From the passenger seat, you can feel that the ride has been firmed up. The Sport doesn't float over larger undulations, nor does it absorb smaller bumps like the Range Rover can, but it seems to stay flatter under cornering. You can tell that the steering has been made more direct too, as you get moved about by smaller corrections made on the road, although your head isn't forced to nod about like it does in the previous-generation Range Rover.

The Sport has a smaller underbody skid plate and different exhaust design to the larger car, which certainly allows more engine noise to permeate the cabin. This means the driver feels more involved with what the car is doing, and passengers get a

**ABOVE**
Pre-production car still wears heavy camouflage, but Range Rover Evoque-inspired styling cues are evident in the front grille, headlights and tail-lamps. Sport shares its architecture with the new Range Rover, unlike the previous generation, which was based on the Discovery 3

**RIGHT**
Electronic stability control keeps the Sport pointing in the right direction on even the slipperiest surfaces. But keen drivers can reduce its effect simply by switching to Dynamic driving mode, which allows the back end to move around and makes the steering, throttle and brakes more responsive

"The Sport's Terrain Response 2 system is designed to take you where no other car can go"

VX12 OCP

Snow, ice, and the deep-frozen winter of the Arctic Circle are just part of a rigorous testing process for the Range Rover Sport. By making sure the car works in such extreme conditions - whether here or in scorching, sandy desert heat, Land Rover knows that it will be able to cope with anything that owners throw at it, even if most examples will spend the majority of time on Tarmac roads in temperate climates rather than extreme off-road environments

"Sport always feels like it has rock-solid grip, even as the road surface changes from deep, fluffy snow to harsh black ice"

BELOW
Sport shares the
top of its dashboard
with the Range Rover,
but lower section
slopes more and
smaller steering
wheel feels sportier

BOTTOM
Dynamic mode adds
a red ring to the
Sport's digital
dials, while display
between the speedo
and rev counter shows
the selected gear

stronger sense of the impressive acceleration. Traction seemed strong out on the polished-ice surface of the lake, with the Sport clinging on well thanks to subtle interventions from the stability control. At higher speeds, predictable understeer creeps in.

Part of this confident performance is down to the new Torque Vectoring By Braking (TVBB) system, which uses the brakes on all four wheels to help shuffle torque to the one that needs it most, giving more grip when cornering. The system also locks up the rear differential imperceptibly, helping you to accelerate out of a bend. The effect is not as sharp as you'll get in a Porsche Cayenne, but the Sport has a more forgiving ride.

The upshot of all of this is that the new Range Rover Sport always feels like it has rock-solid grip, even as the road surface changes from deep, fluffy snow to sections of harsh black ice when we head north. With the dark snow clouds clearing and the temperature dropping to minus 11 degrees, we stop to take some photos at a sign marking the edge of the Arctic Circle.

The Terrain Response 2 system is designed to allow you to drive where no other car can go, yet even those drivers who don't venture far off-road will be glad to have it. Over 100 miles later, we reach the end of our road trip as we approach the Norwegian border. The terrain is a patchwork of snow and ice, and the Sport automatically switches between its normal, grass, gravel and snow settings numerous times.

Yet you wouldn't know this was happening, unless you noticed the light illuminating on the dash informing you the stop-start system is inactive. It's the reassurance that the technology has been refined in the cold, snowy wastes of Sweden that promises to make the new Range Rover Sport seriously impress drivers, wherever they choose to take it.

And the cold-weather testing up here is just one part of the Sport's long development story. After fine-tuning their imperious grip in the biting cold, snow and ice, the test cars head to Dubai for testing in the sandy desert in temperatures of over 50 degrees. After that comes Utah in the United States, where ability to tackle dry, rocky terrain is honed. Add to that countless miles closer to home in the UK, and the new car looks like it will set new standards for how far a Range Rover Sport can go – whether you're on or off the beaten track. LR

# ROYAL ROVERS

Sixty glorious years on and the Land Rover brand is still a firm fixture in Queen Elizabeth II's fleet. We look back at the very special vehicles that have received the Royal seal of approval

You wouldn't expect Her Majesty the Queen to admit to having a favourite car company, but the fact that Land Rover is the only car manufacturer with four Royal Warrants probably says all that you need to know about how fond she is of the brand.

Land Rover has been supplying cars to the Queen throughout her 60-year reign, so the opportunity for us to drive a few of the more famous examples around her back garden, Windsor Great Park, is a suitable tribute to the close relationship that exists between the monarch and the brand.

The Queen had been on the throne for just a couple of years (and Land Rover making cars for a mere six) when a Series I was adapted to enable the new Defender of the Faith to stand in the back of the car while she waved at her subjects during her six-month tour of the Commonwealth. It was the first ever Royal Land Rover, and was christened State IV.

Now, almost 60 years later, the unregistered car looks as smart as it ever did, with its Royal-claret paintwork. The driver and front-passenger seats do seem a little more careworn, with cracked blue leather and a rather well-used look to the cockpit. But once you've slid yourself behind the oversized, skinny-rimmed steering wheel, it's surprising how comfortable the driving position actually is - not traditionally a strong point of

## "Although there are leaning supports, being in the back of State IV must have been like riding a rodeo horse"

old Land Rovers. You need a bit of choke to start the car, and a firm hand to select first, but State IV is relatively easy to drive.

Even so, it's no wonder that the driver looks nervous in photos when the Queen is on board. Because of the unassisted brakes, the heavy steering, clunky gearbox and sensitive throttle, driving the car smoothly is a real art. Her Majesty and Prince Phillip had to remain skilled at staying upright, with one hand in the air, as the car drove through the crowds. Although there are handily placed and beautifully trimmed seats, and leaning supports in the back of the car, it must have been like riding a rodeo horse at times, thanks to a ride that's best described as 'bouncy'.

State IV accompanied the Queen on a tour that covered Australia and New Zealand, Sri Lanka (then Ceylon), Yemen (Aden) Africa and Europe, and was used for Royal events up until 1974.

State II, meanwhile – another Royal ceremonial vehicle – was built in 1958 in the jig shop at Land Rover's factory in Solihull. This was an 88-inch model, two inches bigger than State IV; it was

finished in the same claret paint, with a blue-leather interior and blue lenses for the side lamps, to indicate that the car was a Royal vehicle. State II was a reserve car kept at Land Rover HQ, so has just 13,000 miles on the beautifully retro odometer.

In 1974 the Queen was presented with State I, her latest Royal ceremonial Land Rover. This time based on a standard three-door Range Rover, State I was made without a roof, tailgate or side windows. The bulkhead behind the driver was shifted forward, and the exhaust was moved from the back of the car so that the Royal passengers wouldn't have to smell exhaust fumes.

The Queen's quarters still look regal today: they're trimmed in brown leather with fold-down seats, and some half seats to lean on. There's even a lectern in the bulkhead, and a couple of cleverly concealed umbrellas in case of rain. Up front, the Royal driver is also spoiled. The big leather bench is as comfy as it looks, while the header rail is leather-trimmed and has a special spoiler to prevent Her Majesty from being buffeted.

As we drive out into Windsor Great Park, the ungainly looking Range Rover stops passersby in their tracks, despite the fact that the Royal Standard isn't currently flying from the chrome flag holder located in the middle of the bonnet.

Inside, the clash of the leather with the stark, 1970s plastic steering wheel and dash looks a little odd, but the V8 engine fires up cleanly with a beautiful rumble, the gearshift feels reasonably precise and the throttle is less sensitive than that of State IV. Life is not only more comfortable for the driver, thanks to much easier steering, but the ride is more supple and forgiving: better for Royal wavers in the back.

We also took the opportunity to get behind the wheel of the late Queen Mother's favourite car: NLT 9, a 1995 Range Rover LSE. This much more modern Range Rover is still quite original; it's finished in Ardennes Green, with only large side steps added to enable the Queen Mother to easily get into the back.

The 4.2-litre V8 burbles along beautifully, with power-steering and an auto 'box making it really easy to drive. However, in true old Range Rover style, there are warning lights on the dash and the driver's electric seat controls don't work - it seems that Royal cars aren't immune to electrical gremlins.

The Queen still uses a Range Rover: her 58-plate model, complete with chrome flag holder and bonnet-mounted motif, collected her from 2012's Diamond Jubilee Pageant in Windsor.

Officially, of course, Land Rover won't discuss any deals that it conducts with the Royals, but we are told that the Queen buys her cars these days. Not that you can expect to find Her Majesty in your local Land Rover dealership at any time soon.

**CLOCKWISE FROM LEFT**
State IV, adapted from a Series I Land Rover, is decked out in Royal claret with a blue leather interior; Her Majesty driving her current car, a 58-plate Range Rover; the Queen and the Duke of Edinburgh inspect a military parade in Hyde Park from the back of State IV, during 1953

| 94bhp | 250lb ft at 0rpm | 0g/km | 2162kg |
|-------|------------------|--------|--------|
| POWER | TORQUE | CO2 | KERBWEIGHT |

# FULLY CHARGED

Underneath the traditional exterior of this Defender is an all-electric drivetrain that will help shape the future of Land Rover's low and emission-free vehicles´

**JUST IN CASE ANYONE** thought the Defender was a bit of an anachronism, seven fully electric 110s appeared at the Geneva Motor Show earlier this year, where they generated as much of a stir as the new Range Rover did. It is a clever, relevant piece of work that demonstrates Land Rover's intent to build vehicles with low and zero carbon emissions and, although it won't get built, it points to the possibility of a Land Rover powered solely by electricity.

And it is a proper Land Rover, too. A big part of the programme was producing a vehicle that would retain the Defender's off-road capability. In fact, the conversion has improved how the Defender deals with some rough terrain including (and yes, it does sound a little unlikely) deep water.

That's because the motor, battery and power electrics are totally waterproof, unlike a combustion engine. It will wade to 800mm, 200mm deeper than a normal Defender and, in theory, you could submerge the whole vehicle and it would carry on. To do that with a combustion-engined Land Rover you need to

ALL-TERRAIN
ELECTRIC
RESEARCH VEHICLE

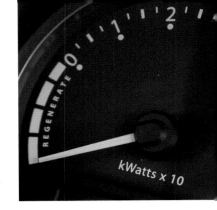

do a lot of preparation. An electric drivetrain doesn't require an air intake or an exhaust, either. And much of the cooling is done by siting the battery under the bonnet, in the engine's place, which is the best place to put it to take advantage of air flow through the vehicle.

The genesis of this vehicle came from a fairly unforgiving environment - the African bush. A South African safari company wanted a quiet vehicle that wouldn't disturb wildlife, so they commissioned an electric Defender. That had a top speed of 40mph, but could hit that in forward and reverse, which gave it an edge if the driver needed to escape a charging elephant and the only way out was backwards.

This Defender is more sophisticated. It can do 70mph, and has more torque - 250lb ft, 110 per cent more at high speeds, which makes it quicker to 60mph. Its motor, sandwiched between the engine and transfer box is simple in construction, relatively small but capable of producing a high torque figure.

The fact that all the torque is available from 0rpm makes it even more effective off-road, where low-down shove is much more relevant than outright power.

You don't need to change gear or balance a clutch, either, because it has a single speed reduction gear, allowing it to creep over obstacles using just the accelerator to control momentum. Land Rover reckons

it will do eight hours of low-speed off-road use on a full charge, which takes 10 hours - or four if you're using a high-voltage charger. Regenerative braking means it can recover up to 80 per cent of the kinetic energy produced by the vehicle.

In the cab it's all pretty much standard, apart from a new panel with a big kill switch and, in a first for the Defender, the controls for Terrain Response and Hill Descent Control.

You won't be able to buy one: the electric Defenders are test beds for Land Rover's electric drivetrain

## You could submerge the whole vehicle and it could carry on

technology, to show that it's possible to build an off-roader powered by batteries and a motor. One is in use at The Eden Project in Cornwall, pulling a land train to move visitors around the site. Land Rover describes it as a "rolling laboratory to innovate new ideas," and it's part of a long-term strategy to develop electric vehicles. And the first of those will be the hybrid version of the Range Rover Sport, which is coming in about a year's time.

## Plugged in to the future

So with all this talk of the new Range Rover Sport, why are you looking at the previous model? Because this car is a crucial step in the development of Land Rover's hybrid powertrains, and a glimpse at the company's future. It is a plug-in hybrid Range Rover, and the technology that it demonstrates will influence the firm's first production hybrid drivetrain, which will be launched in the new Sport.

Built purely as an experimental vehicle, the Range_e uses a 3.0-litre V6 diesel and a 69Kw motor fitted into the gearbox in place of the torque convertor. It retains the rest of the Sport's transmission, so it has permanent four-wheel drive, a low-ratio option and a locking centre differential. But unlike the electric Defender, the Range_e was built to operate as effectively on-road as off it. So it's capable of doing most low-speed urban work using the electric motor only (in fact, the motor is capable of powering the car

**TOP**
The rev counter in the Defender is replaced by a dial showing how much energy is being used (or generated.)

by itself up to 70mph), which goes a long way towards its impressively low $CO_2$ figure of 89g/km.

The crucial difference between this car and the Sport hybrid we'll get next year is that this one can be plugged in to charge the battery. The Sport hybrid's battery will be charged from the car's regenerative braking and other energy recovery technology. But Land Rover is working at putting plug-in hybrid technology into its cars expect to see it in a production Land Rover within the next three years.  LR

## The technology in the Range_e will influence the production hybrid

# EVOLUTION OF THE SPECIES

There have only been four generations of Range Rover since 1970. From the iconic original to the groundbreaking new model, we examine how each one shaped and redefined the legend

Styling has changed
with the times and
the technology has
advanced almost
beyond recognition,
but the core Range
Rover values that
were present on
day one remain:
imperious off-road
capability, supreme
luxury and bluff,
distinguished looks
unlike any other
car on the road

| 1970-1994 | £19,980 | 3458cc/V8 | 135 | 185lb/ft |
|-----------|---------|-----------|-----|----------|
| PRODUCTION | PRICE NEW | ENGINE | BHP | TORQUE |

# ENDURING HERITAGE

## Rover's decision to combine the comfort of its cars with the toughness of a Land Rover created a motoring icon

**IF YOU GATHER** opinion on what was the first true Sport Utility Vehicle, you'll come up against two intractable camps. One (generally American) maintains it must be the 1963 Jeep Wagoneer. The other (mostly everyone else) says Range Rover.

Thing is, the Wagoneer was a big estate with optional four-wheel drive. Jeep didn't market it as an off-road vehicle and it wasn't until the second generation that it even started to look like a 4x4. The original Range Rover, however, was always going to be a proper off-roader. Taller than the Wagoneer, with styling that owed less to a traditional American 'station wagon' and more to a new, brave and unconventional concept of what a car could be.

But it didn't appear instantly, from a sparkle of inspiration. Rover had long been trying to design a utility vehicle combining the practicality of a Land Rover (then seen as a commercial vehicle) with the comfort of its passenger cars. Some awkward prototypes emerged in the late fifties, but they were not much more than big estates, based on two-wheel-drive car chassis, like the Wagoneer.

So Rover started from scratch. A fresh vehicle with a new chassis and suspension emerged – a large estate with more ground clearance, permanent four-wheel drive and a big V8. It had to be superlative off-road and comfortable on it, so it had long-travel coil springs that gave superb axle articulation and an absorbent ride.

The styling was almost an accident. A body was needed for the test mules, so engineers knocked up a shell before the designers sorted the final look. But everyone preferred it to what the stylists were working on, and it got the green light. This is what made the Range Rover look right - not so much function dictating form, but function and form becoming one in the hands of the engineers.

Function was an important part of what the first Range Rovers were about. They were utility vehicles with plastic seats and floor coverings, so you could hose them out. The car in our pictures is a later vehicle, from 1982 - about the time Range Rover assumed the upmarket position it holds today. Look closely and you'll see it has a Vogue badge - as in Vogue, the high-end fashion magazine.

The story of how it commissioned a one-off Range Rover for a photo shoot, giving Land Rover the confidence to produce a limited-edition model, is well known. It symbolises the moment the Range Rover became more than a comfortable car that was good at towing. It doesn't sound like much today, but this Vogue has air-conditioning, walnut trim, a decent stereo and masses of carpet - at a time when heated rear screens were usually optional.

The Range Rover became more expensive, better equipped and increasingly desirable over time. It grew more sophisticated, with air-suspension and anti-lock brakes, but the styling remained. And even when the replacement arrived, the Classic (as it became known) stayed in production for two years. Not bad for a car that some Rover executives originally believed had no future.

BELOW
This 1982 Vogue model shows the start of the Range Rover's transition from a utilitarian work vehicle to rugged luxury car. Wood trim, thick carpets and air-conditioning were all unheard of in off-road vehicles until this point

### THE LONG ROAD TO THE RANGE ROVER
#### ROAD ROVER 1 1951

"This is what made the Range Rover look right: function and form becoming one"

Yes, it looks like it was designed by a child, but this crude, boxy creation is where the idea of a more car-like utility vehicle started. The first Road Rover, from 1951, was a simple estate car based on a Rover P4, and it was two-wheel drive, Although the idea was well received within Rover, the project was shelved, because the Land Rover was doing so well. But the concept of a more civilised utility vehicle didn't go away...

| 1994-2002 | £31,950 | 3950cc/V8 | 177 | 221lb/ft |
|-----------|---------|-----------|-----|----------|
| PRODUCTION | PRICE NEW | ENGINE | BHP | TORQUE |

# WORTH THE WAIT

It was a long time coming, but the second-generation P38 proved capable of continuing the Classic's legacy

**IMAGINE A CAR** company today waiting 24 years to replace a model. That's how long it took for the second-generation Range Rover, codenamed P38, to appear. To put it into context, it's like the second-generation car – which was launched in 1994 – still being on sale today, with the brand-new model not showing up until 2017. A tricky one to pull off: by 1994, the Range Rover was established as the best car of its kind, already well on its way to perfecting the combination of limousine comfort and all-terrain mastery that has remained its unique selling point to this day.

And while it doesn't seem so radical now, the P38 was a big moment in Range Rover history - the first time the iconic original shape had been changed. The Classic had filled out a little over the years, but it still fundamentally looked like the same vehicle from the outside. Now, it was about to become something different.

For the first time, the original Range Rover design elements - the 'floating' roof, the castellated clamshell bonnet, the relationship of the glass to the body - were evolved and translated into a new look. The P38 softened the original car's slab-sided flanks and panels, updating but not recklessly modernising them into a softer, sleeker shape that also greatly improved the car's aerodynamics.

Inside, things became much more sophisticated. The Range Rover now had a cabin that could match the very best big executive saloons such as the BMW 7 Series and Mercedes S-Class. As well as a large centre stack full of buttons and gadgets, it had a driving position closer to a car's than the Classic model had ever managed.

It wasn't quite so much of a departure underneath: the new car was still built on a conventional steel ladder-frame chassis, with live axles and coil springs. But there was the option of air-suspension on both axles, which raised the ride height and improved the Range Rover's already impressive off-road ability.

Power still came from the venerable Rover V8 engine, although Land Rover's engineers had by now managed to get 4.6 litres out of it. A modern diesel engine was also offered - a proper six-cylinder turbo sourced from BMW instead of the thumping old four-cylinder from the Classic. It wasn't quite powerful enough to give the Range Rover the sort of eye-opening on-road performance owners have come to expect these days, but it massively improved refinement and fuel consumption compared to the old car.

History hasn't quite worked out what to make of the P38 Range Rover yet. Seen within the context of the most recent version, it probably seems like a bit of a stopgap – a mid-point between the inspired genius of the original and the hi-tech, luxurious modernism of newer versions. In the context of its time, however, it was a very desirable product that definitely upheld the dual-purpose philosophy of its predecessor well. So, on reflection can it be considered a 'proper' Range Rover? Very much so.

**BELOW**
With the arrival of the second-generation P38 in 1994, the Range Rover's status as an alternative to executive saloons was consolidated. An up-to-date cabin matched the best BMW or Mercedes offered when it came to fit, finish and equipment

**THE LONG ROAD TO THE RANGE ROVER**
**ROAD ROVER 2 1958**

"All of the original Range Rover design elements were evolved into a new look"

A more successful attempt at a useful wagon, using Rover P5 mechanicals. Rover wanted to market the Road Rover as a car, not a Land Rover. And with independent front suspension and front disc brakes, it was closer to its cars. The Road Rover came close to production, with a launch date of 1960. But Rover had to deal with the upcoming P6 saloon and developing the Land Rover, so the Road Rover was put aside.

| 2002-2013 | £45,995 | 4398cc/V8 | 282 | 324lb/ft |
|-----------|---------|-----------|-----|----------|
| PRODUCTION | PRICE NEW | ENGINE | BHP | TORQUE |

# MODERN CLASSIC

A decade after first re-inventing an icon, Land Rover did it again – bringing the Range Rover into the 21st century

**THIS IS WHERE THE** the Range Rover really got into its stride. It's easy to get carried away talking about cars that redefine their classes, but the extraordinary third-generation L322 Range Rover managed that not-inconsiderable task with ease.

Look at it. Yes, we're all a bit too familiar with its appearance by now, but go on, really look at it. It manages to combine an imposing presence with classic Range Rover style. It incorporates all the brand's key elements without getting bogged down in pastiche, successfully mixing elegance with substance. And, after 11 years on the market, it's not even beginning to look dated. It simply looks just like a Range Rover should.

And then there's the cabin, which must have caused moments of panic in Mercedes' interior design studio when it first appeared. The structure is almost architectural, with aluminium spars, clean lines and clever materials throughout. It was new, fresh, upmarket and – above all – unique. There were no overstated retro flourishes. You could have bamboo instead of burr walnut, and the wooden trim looked like it was holding up the dashboard, rather than just hanging on to it. Shut the door, and you were in another world.

And the bits you couldn't see came from another world, too – especially when compared to the dated underpinnings of the previous car. Power initially came from BMW-sourced petrol and diesel V8s, but Land Rover soon replaced these with Jaguar-developed engines. The finest was the supercharged V8, which was an absolute gem of an engine: refined and easy-going at low speeds but capable of launching the Range Rover up the road at a shocking rate. It also made a great noise, and its mix of performance with an imperious nature created the most complete Range Rover yet.

Most importantly, the car was a built on a platform that could deal with that kind of performance. The separate chassis was gone, replaced by a monocoque that gave the Range Rover new-found refinement. Combined with fully independent suspension, it gave the car the true limousine-like ride it had always aspired to. It rolls a bit in corners, but it also soaks up all sorts of nasty road surfaces – absorbing, cosseting and generally keeping passengers relaxed.

Independent suspension is generally thought to be inferior to beam axles for off-road use, as when one wheel is pushed up by a rock or other object, its opposite number isn't pushed down to compensate, leaving the car unstable. To rectify this, the L322 has connected air-suspension that compensates for wheel movement.

Rather than being a compromise, this actually made the Range Rover even more capable in the rough. Combined with the first version of Land Rover's electronic Terrain Response traction-control system, it made the L322 almost unstoppable off-road. Good enough to better even the legendary Defender, in fact.

So is the L322 the most complete model Range Rover ever made? Definitely. Well, it was until about three months ago...

**THE LONG ROAD TO THE RANGE ROVER**
**100-INCH STATION WAGON 1967**

"It's not even beginning to look dated. It simply looks like a Range Rover should"

**LEFT**
Aluminium spars and bamboo wood trim were among the fresh new elements to grace the L322's impressive cabin. It remained the last word in refinement and luxury, without getting bogged down in a staid attempt to recreate the classic model's past glories

This is where it started to get significantly more considered, and the ingredients that became the Range Rover really gain definition. So it has long-travel coil-sprung suspension, permanent four-wheel drive, Rover's V8 and an aluminium body bolted to a steel frame. It's shown here with the cars Rover considered as competition, including (oddly) a Mini Countryman and Land Rover's own 88-inch Station Wagon.

| 2013- PRODUCTION | £84,320 PRICE NEW | 4367cc/V8 ENGINE | 335 BHP | 516lb/ft TORQUE |
|---|---|---|---|---|

# A LEGEND EVOLVED

## Bristling with technology and attention to detail, the new Range Rover is the most stylish and capable yet

**AT THIS POINT** in the car's life, trying to design a new Range Rover must be like redesigning the Eiffel Tower. "It has to look like the Eiffel Tower, but it can't just look like the Eiffel Tower," the design brief would say. "Instantly recognisable, yet totally different. Keep all the important bits, but make it look totally up-to-date."

So this is what Land Rover came up with. If you think the last model was futuristic, this looks like a spaceship. It makes cars around it seem like they're from the last century. You'd need the drama of a Ferrari to take attention from this Range Rover, such is its intense modernism. Neat styling disguises its size: a narrow glasshouse, what looks like a like a sloping roof (actually a rising waistline) and fine detailing conspire to reduce its apparent mass.

But crucially, it's still a Range Rover. Take the badges off and everyone would still know what it is – even with new elements like the sloping grille and the top of the rear lights wrapping around into the body. It's arguably a bolder change than the previous car.

The cabin's clean look has been developed into something even sleeker and more high-end. It's still very modern, clean and neat, without being clinical. The trim inserts still look structural – whether aluminium, wood or glossy black lacquer. Every part seems considered and purposeful. Yet one of the Range Rover's cleverest qualities is how it seems to shrink around the driver. It's a large car, but rarely feels too large, such is the way the driving position lets you see and sense its extremities. And that makes it surprisingly easy to place on the road or thread into a parking space - you're never struggling to figure out where the corners are.

Steering and handling are deceptively light, too. Like a Jaguar XJ, the new Range Rover's agility belies its size. You can easily hustle it across roads that seem far too tight or contorted for a car as big as this. It doesn't roll or meander, it just sits planted on the road – all grip, traction and assured control. And while it's doing all of this, it's soaking up every pothole and rut you can find, and damping any crashy, shuddering vibrations that might detract from your or your passengers' comfort. This is why people say the Range Rover is the best all-round luxury car in the world.

A lot of work has gone into making the car behave like this. It's mainly what you can't see, like the incredibly stiff and strong aluminium monocoque, the aluminium suspension components and all-new air-suspension. There's also Dynamic Response, which is a highly effective electronic anti-roll bar that was developed on British roads, so it's well suited to poor surfaces.

That's what the latest Range Rover is made of – technology and strength wrapped in an ultra-modern cloak. It's capable of fording a river, whisking its occupants across continents or just cruising around town. Back in the mid-sixties, when the concept of the car was being defined, this is exactly what the engineers had in mind.

**BELOW**
All-new car has been restyled just as comprehensively inside, and once again sets the luxury standard

**THE LONG ROAD TO THE RANGE ROVER**
**ROAD ROVER 1 1951**

"It's a Range Rover. Take the badges off and everyone would still know what it is"

The final models still bore the name Road Rover but the overall design had been finalised. This picture shows that Rover was working through alternative grille and light treatments, but everything else had

been worked out. The styling evolved a little further to become the final prototypes, which were badged Velar.

# AHEAD OF THE GAME

As far back as 1949, Land Rover experimented with adding luxury to its rugged off-roader. The result was the Tickford Station Wagon. Buyers weren't sure what to make of it, but it turned out to be way ahead of its time

**ABOVE**
The advertising tagline for the Tickford Station Wagon read "Meets any occasion." It would be equally at home collecting guests from the train station or working on the farm

**THE TICKFORD STATION** Wagon was a very early attempt to add comfort to the original Land Rover, which, even by the standards of the day, was a fairly uncomfortable way to travel. It was pitched to buyers as a sort of go-anywhere people carrier, and one that was somewhat smarter than a regular Land Rover. The car's advertising tag line was "meets any occasion".

It had a coachbuilt body (made by Tickford, hence the name), wind-up windows, carpets and one-piece doors – all comforts that the basic standard Land Rover most certainly didn't have. So, was the Tickford ahead of its time? Well, yes – the idea of adding luxury to a four-wheel-drive utility vehicle to increase its appeal and day-to-day usability was a clever one.

And there simply weren't that many four-wheel-drive vehicles around in 1949 – in the UK you had the choice of either a Land Rover or a Jeep left over from the war. That was it. The Tickford was very much the first and only vehicle of its type – rather like the original Range Rover was in 1970.

The problem with the Tickford Station Wagon was its high purchase price. At £959, it cost £109 more than a normal Land Rover, and back then buyers were simply not prepared to pay that much for what was still regarded as a commercial vehicle. Few were sold, and after a year Tickford knocked the Station Wagon on the head.

That makes this car a rare and very pricey collector's item today. Examples in good condition fetch over £30,000 – which, oddly enough, is pretty much equivalent to the Tickford's original retail price in today's money. Recognition, perhaps, that it was simply the right car at the wrong time.

**ABOVE**
Large coachbuilt body gives the Tickford an unmistakable profile. It was a slow seller when launched, but has gone on to become a rare and desirable version of the classic Land Rover

# CONCEPT TO REALITY

Few cars make it from futuristic concept to full production virtually unchanged, but that's just what happened with the Range Rover Evoque. We reveal its intriguing journey

**RIGHT**
The bodywork
first comes together
in the factory for
the Tooling Tryout
prototype - it's
the first time the
engineers find
out whether their
calculations are
actually right

So how exactly do you go about making a new car from scratch? We're not talking about a facelift, or turning a hatchback into an estate. We're talking about a completely new model, the like of which the manufacturer has never tried before.

If that isn't enough, this is also to be a new model based on a fairly radical concept car that looks like it's arrived from the future. The idea is to keep the finished product looking more or less the same. Oh yes, and it needs to have road manners approaching those of a sports car, while still managing to be the best in class when off-road. That kind of goes without saying, because the model will be made by Land Rover, and all its cars have to go off-road. Properly.

This, then, is pretty much where the team that developed the Evoque started out. It was, says chief programme engineer David Mitchell, a complex task, partly because of the challenge of the car's packaginf, and also because the idea of a small, rakish, four-seat SUV didn't exist in Land Rover's portfolio before the Evoque; in fact, it didn't really exist anywhere. BMW's X1 was launched prior to the Evoque, but its design and concept are much more conventional than the Land Rover's.

And that's because of the way the Evoque was conceived. In 2006, Land Rover knew it wanted to make a smaller, lighter, sportier car to compete in the growing market of such vehicles. So, during 2007 it produced a concept, the striking LRX, to see the reaction such a vehicle would get, and displayed it at the Detroit Show in 2008. That's not unusual – the job of a concept is to gauge opinion – but what is unusual, especially for Land Rover, is that the concept came before any development had begun. If a concept car is going to make production, generally it already has before it appears. But here the LRX was the actual idea.

Once the LRX's design had been signed off, and Mitchell and his team had worked out that yes, it

would be possible to turn it into a real car, they started to build the first engineering test vehicles. These are officially called X1 cars, but are more informally known as go-karts, as they have no bodywork and are just a platform with a drivetrain – just like a go-kart, in fact. They're used to check that the layout and balance of the car isn't completely wrong.

The Evoque had another crucial component that required early testing: its MagneRide dampers. These are filled with a magnetically charged fluid that can be made thicker or thinner with an electrical charge, in order to change the car's ride characteristics. It's not new technology, but employing it in a car that can wade through deep water, and be used properly off-road, is new. And Land Rover needed to know it would work.

Engineering the Evoque's off-road capability was one of the biggest challenges of the project, says David Mitchell. A proper off-road vehicle is subjected to much higher loads than a normal car; everything gets put under more stress, so it must be stronger than average. The trouble is that strength can add weight, and one of the guiding principles of the Evoque project was to cut as much mass as possible. The use of strong, lightweight materials is the solution, but they're often expensive. The balance is a fine one, and requires elegant solutions. Most rival manufacturers don't have to face the same issues, as their vehicles aren't designed to venture as far off-road: they're not subjected to the sort of loads that a Land Rover must cope with.

Which is why the Evoque has plastic wings, an aluminium roof panel and a plastic tailgate. Mitchell says that they looked into using a steel tailgate, but that the weight gain over plastic couldn't be offset anywhere else; they had a target of saving 100kg from the weight of the Freelander on which the Evoque is loosely based.

By this point, testing had moved on to the next stage of prototype, called M1. These are the test mules that you see in car magazines, which often look like a current model, but have chopped-about bodywork and strange ride heights. The Evoque M1 cars wore a modified Freelander shell – although the finished design was pretty much sorted, because of the desire to replicate the LRX as a production car. Normally, says Mitchell, at this stage you might have several design prototypes under test, and it's at this point that you make a choice. But with the

**LEFT AND MAIN IMAGE**
Cold-chamber testing is a vital part of new-model development; it allows engineers to ensure that all components continue to work even in the most extreme of conditions

**LEFT AND RIGHT**
The Evoque's chief
programme engineer,
David Mitchell,
says that
engineering the
car's vital off-
road capabilities
was one of the
toughest challenges
of the whole project

Evoque there was only one design to consider, and this made the process a lot quicker.

The testing regime is long, arduous, punishing and designed to explore every single component; it's meant to expose any weak point and discover every flaw. So the Evoque was sent to Dubai to be cooked in the desert while climbing the monster sand dune known as Big Red, in temperatures greater than 50 degrees Celsius. It went to the Nürburgring to be driven harder and faster than any owner would ever dare, and to the Nardo track in Italy for sustained high-speed testing. It went to Death Valley and towed huge loads across the Hoover Dam, and had its brakes cooked on the Grossglockner pass in Austria. At its peak, 500 people worked on the project; when the final engineering confirmation stage was reached, they were carrying out 12,000 tests.

These are huge projects, the complexity of modern cars demanding enormous resources . Take the volume of wiring in the Evoque – the harnesses are metres long, and fill most of the space beneath the carpets and boot trim. All of this has to work perfectly all of the time, regardless of how hot or cold it is, or whether the car is driving through a river.

Then they have to build it. Land Rover has a piece of virtual-reality kit nicknamed The Cave, which is used to create detailed projections of car interiors and bodyshells, and just about every assembly that makes up a complete vehicle. They can then be assessed and built up before so much as a door skin is pressed. It saves time and money, and an entire vehicle can be assembled in virtual reality. But even with the accuracy

of The Cave, it's not until the first pre-builds are assembled in the factory (they're known as TT cars, which stands for 'Tooling Tryout') that Mitchell and his team find out whether everything fits together.

"The Cave is good for many things," he says, "but some of the more flexible parts, like the wiring harnesses, are harder to get right." So a small production line is constructed, which mimics the processes that will create the thousands of Evoques to pour off the line at Halewood. It doesn't operate at anything like the speed of the full line, but it does simulate the level of automation required.

Pleasingly, it's not all serious stuff. The creativity of engineers is often forgotten in the techno-rush of specifications, loadings and calculations, but Mitchell and his team formed a kind of skunkworks group to develop what he describes as a 'novelty'. That's not the kind normally associated with cheap children's toys, but playful detailing to set the Evoque apart from its rivals. Mitchell wanted to do something interesting with the downlighting from the door mirrors, and hit upon the idea of projecting a silhouette of the Evoque into the light pool, so it would appear on the ground. If you get the chance to see an Evoque at night, look at the light pool and you'll be able to see that silhouette.

And this, it turns out, is the part of the Evoque that Mitchell likes best. He's chuffed with the way they managed to translate the LRX into a production car, and how they maintained interior space while keeping the low roofline. But you can tell that, on a personal level, it's the silhouette that he's really pleased with.

**RIGHT**
A true off-road
vehicle comes under
much greater stress
than a regular car,
so it's crucial
that the strongest
materials are used,
without weight
being compromised

"All wiring must work perfectly, even when the car is driven through a river"

**LEFT**
The Evoque is fitted with MagneRide dampers, which can be adjusted to change the car's ride characteristics. Early testing by Land Rover proved their efficiency even when the Evoque was taken through water

**THIS IMAGE**
Land Rover produced
the striking LRX
concept in 2007;
it made its debut at
the Detroit Motor
Show the following
year. Right from the
start, the design was
destined to become
production reality

# LRX TO EVOQUE

Turning the LRX into a fully functioning road car
was a true challenge. The LRX was only Land Rover's
second proper concept, and although designed with the
possibility of becoming reality, it still created a new
set of issues and obstacles. "It definitely stretched
us," says David Mitchell. "We didn't know that we could do
it when we first started thinking about it."

Originally, they thought about basing the Evoque on Ford's
C1 platform - the same as that used in the Focus - but they
quickly realised that it wouldn't be a Range Rover. So they
moved to the Freelander, which could give the Evoque the
toughness and performance that it needed.

The Freelander's architecture has been hugely altered
to replicate the LRX's low, short outline, and it was
the height - or lack of it - that resulted in the biggest
changes. To get as close as possible to the LRX's 1535mm
height, the engineers had to squash the structure that
sits directly below the driver's seat and above the

underside of the car. The result is 70mm taller than
the LRX, but 135mm lower than a Freelander.

The Evoque's low roofline and high beltline mean that
it has relatively small pieces of glass - so where do you
put the aerial and telematics equipment that feeds the
GPS? Often it will end up bonded into the glass, but there
wasn't enough surface area here; so they fitted it all into
the rear spoiler instead, preserving the car's looks.

This level of detail extends to the interior. The Evoque
doesn't have conventional roof-mounted grab handles:
the low roofline means that their ideal location would
interfere with the ceiling airbags. The only way of
getting them in would have been to raise the car's roof
height. And it simply wasn't worth compromising the
Evoque's looks for some grab handles.

So no, turning a concept into reality wasn't a simple
process. But aren't you glad that they made the effort?

**LEFT**
Clay models of the Evoque clearly show how true its streamlined styling would remain to that of the LRX concept

**LEFT AND RIGHT**
Initial design sketches for the LRX, which was to become only the second concept car that Land Rover had produced

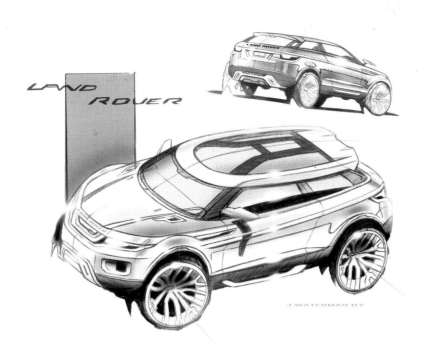

**THIS IMAGE**
The finished product. The Evoque – built on the Freelander's platform – ended up only 70mm taller than the LRX concept

# EVERY LAND ROVER

From basic prototypes to the luxury of the new Range Rover, as well as short and long-wheelbase versions and military vehicles, Land Rover's products have continuously evolved for 65 years

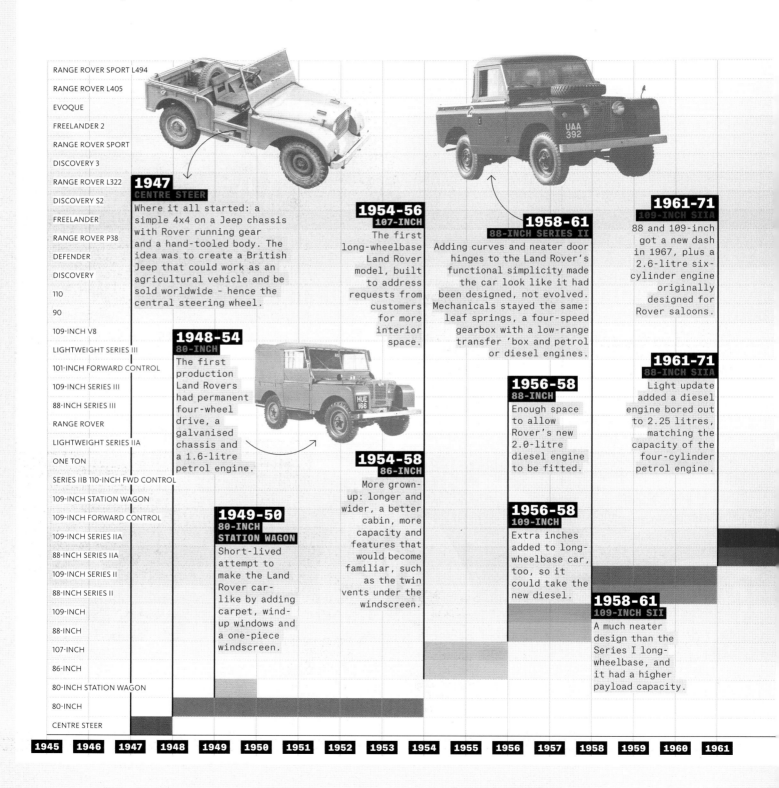

RANGE ROVER SPORT L494
RANGE ROVER L405
EVOQUE
FREELANDER 2
RANGE ROVER SPORT
DISCOVERY 3
RANGE ROVER L322
DISCOVERY S2
FREELANDER
RANGE ROVER P38
DEFENDER
DISCOVERY
110
90
109-INCH V8
LIGHTWEIGHT SERIES III
101-INCH FORWARD CONTROL
109-INCH SERIES III
88-INCH SERIES III
RANGE ROVER
LIGHTWEIGHT SERIES IIA
ONE TON
SERIES IIB 110-INCH FWD CONTROL
109-INCH STATION WAGON
109-INCH FORWARD CONTROL
109-INCH SERIES IIA
88-INCH SERIES IIA
109-INCH SERIES II
88-INCH SERIES II
109-INCH
88-INCH
107-INCH
86-INCH
80-INCH STATION WAGON
80-INCH
CENTRE STEER

**1947**
CENTRE STEER
Where it all started: a simple 4x4 on a Jeep chassis with Rover running gear and a hand-tooled body. The idea was to create a British Jeep that could work as an agricultural vehicle and be sold worldwide - hence the central steering wheel.

**1948-54**
80-INCH
The first production Land Rovers had permanent four-wheel drive, a galvanised chassis and a 1.6-litre petrol engine.

**1949-50**
80-INCH
STATION WAGON
Short-lived attempt to make the Land Rover car-like by adding carpet, wind-up windows and a one-piece windscreen.

**1954-56**
107-INCH
The first long-wheelbase Land Rover model, built to address requests from customers for more interior space.

**1954-58**
86-INCH
More grown-up: longer and wider, a better cabin, more capacity and features that would become familiar, such as the twin vents under the windscreen.

**1958-61**
88-INCH SERIES II
Adding curves and neater door hinges to the Land Rover's functional simplicity made the car look like it had been designed, not evolved. Mechanicals stayed the same: leaf springs, a four-speed gearbox with a low-range transfer 'box and petrol or diesel engines.

**1956-58**
88-INCH
Enough space to allow Rover's new 2.0-litre diesel engine to be fitted.

**1956-58**
109-INCH
Extra inches added to long-wheelbase car, too, so it could take the new diesel.

**1958-61**
109-INCH SII
A much neater design than the Series I long-wheelbase, and it had a higher payload capacity.

**1961-71**
109-INCH SIIA
88 and 109-inch got a new dash in 1967, plus a 2.6-litre six-cylinder engine originally designed for Rover saloons.

**1961-71**
88-INCH SIIA
Light update added a diesel engine bored out to 2.25 litres, matching the capacity of the four-cylinder petrol engine.

1945 | 1946 | 1947 | 1948 | 1949 | 1950 | 1951 | 1952 | 1953 | 1954 | 1955 | 1956 | 1957 | 1958 | 1959 | 1960 | 1961

**1966-72**
**SERIES IIB**
**FORWARD**
**CONTROL**

Improved
on original
design with
more robust
axles, front
anti-roll bar
and a more
powerful
2.6 engine.

**1970-94**
**RANGE ROVER**

After the 1947 original,
this is Land Rover's most
significant vehicle.
Original, versatile and
desirable, it created a new
kind of car and a market for
it. Often referred to as one
of the most influential cars
of all time.

**1972-84**
**LIGHTWEIGHT**
**SERIES III**

SIII upgrades
for the
Airportable.

**1968**
**LIGHTWEIGHT**

Officially
called the
Airportable,
it had
detachable
bodywork,
allowing it to
be airlifted
by the army.

**1962-71**
**109-INCH STATION WAGON**

The first Land Rover with
a 12-seat configuration
was offered in 1962, and
although squeezing 12
passengers inside would have
been a challenge, it allowed
the Land Rover to officially
be classed as a bus and
therefore avoid purchase tax
in the UK.

**1972-78**
**101-INCH**
**FWD CONTROL**

Military model;
Range Rover
running gear.

**1979-83**
**88 AND 109-INCH V8**

V8 power finally arrived
in the Land Rover in 1979
with the Stage One, which
used the Range Rover's
drivetrain. A handful
of 88-inch V8s were
built for export, most
going to Trinidad.

**1971-84**
**109-INCH**
**SERIES III**

All-synchro
gearbox and a
more civilised
cabin added.

**1962-66**
**109-INCH**
**FWD CONTROL**

Moving the cab
forwards so
it sat over the
engine created
a commercial
vehicle with
more space.

**1968-71**
**ONE-TON**

Rare uprated
version of
109-inch,
with a one-
ton payload
and heavily
upgraded
mechanicals.

**1971-83**
**88-INCH**
**SERIES III**

Series IIIs
also got a
stronger five-
bearing engine.

| 1962 | 1963 | 1964 | 1965 | 1966 | 1967 | 1968 | 1969 | 1970 | 1971 | 1972 | 1973 | 1974 | 1975 | 1976 | 1977 | 1978 | 1979 |

RANGE ROVER SPORT 2

RANGE ROVER L405

EVOQUE

FREELANDER 2

RANGE ROVER SPORT

DISCOVERY 3

RANGE ROVER L322

DISCOVERY S2

FREELANDER

RANGE ROVER P38

DEFENDER

DISCOVERY

110-INCH

90-INCH

109-INCH V8

LIGHTWEIGHT SERIES III

101-INCH FORWARD CONTROL

109-INCH SERIES III

88-INCH SERIES III

RANGE ROVER

LIGHTWEIGHT SERIES IIA

ONE TON

SERIES IIB 110-INCH FWD. CONTROL

109-INCH STATION WAGON

109-INCH FORWARD CONTROL

109-INCH SERIES IIA

88-INCH SERIES IIA

109-INCH SERIES II

88-INCH SERIES II

109-INCH

88-INCH

107-INCH

86-INCH

80-INCH STATION WAGON

80-INCH

CENTRE STEER

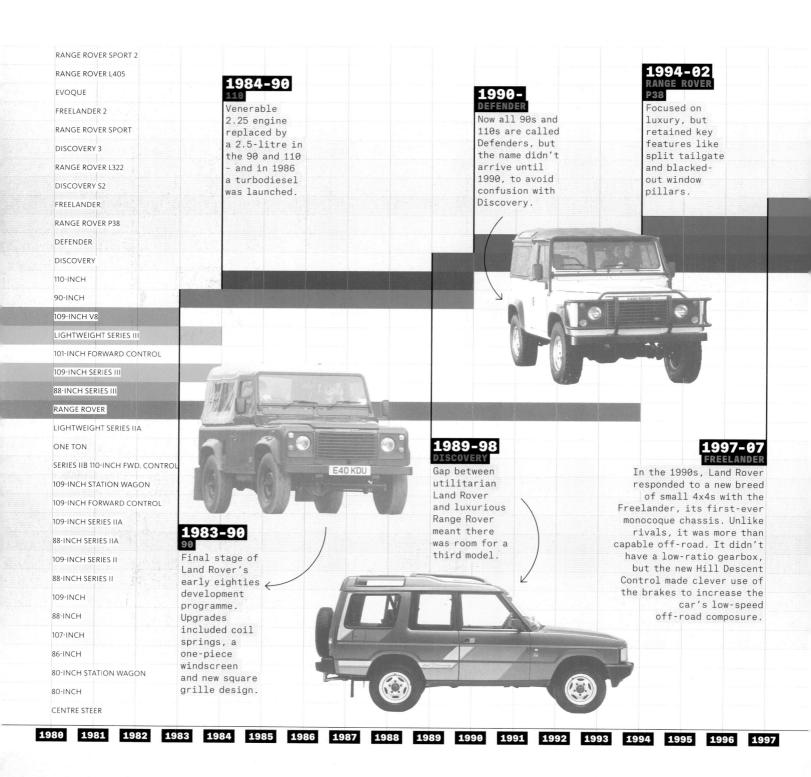

**1984-90**
110
Venerable 2.25 engine replaced by a 2.5-litre in the 90 and 110 – and in 1986 a turbodiesel was launched.

**1990-**
DEFENDER
Now all 90s and 110s are called Defenders, but the name didn't arrive until 1990, to avoid confusion with Discovery.

**1994-02**
RANGE ROVER
P38
Focused on luxury, but retained key features like split tailgate and blacked-out window pillars.

**1983-90**
90
Final stage of Land Rover's early eighties development programme. Upgrades included coil springs, a one-piece windscreen and new square grille design.

**1989-98**
DISCOVERY
Gap between utilitarian Land Rover and luxurious Range Rover meant there was room for a third model.

**1997-07**
FREELANDER
In the 1990s, Land Rover responded to a new breed of small 4x4s with the Freelander, its first-ever monocoque chassis. Unlike rivals, it was more than capable off-road. It didn't have a low-ratio gearbox, but the new Hill Descent Control made clever use of the brakes to increase the car's low-speed off-road composure.

| 1980 | 1981 | 1982 | 1983 | 1984 | 1985 | 1986 | 1987 | 1988 | 1989 | 1990 | 1991 | 1992 | 1993 | 1994 | 1995 | 1996 | 1997 |

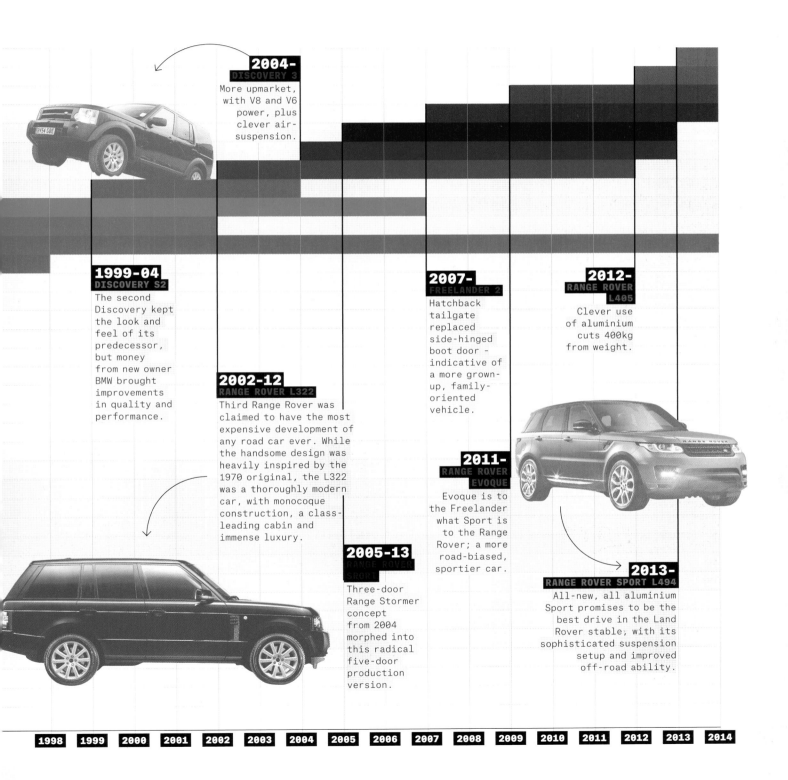

**2004-**
DISCOVERY 3

More upmarket, with V8 and V6 power, plus clever air-suspension.

**1999-04**
DISCOVERY S2

The second Discovery kept the look and feel of its predecessor, but money from new owner BMW brought improvements in quality and performance.

**2002-12**
RANGE ROVER L322

Third Range Rover was claimed to have the most expensive development of any road car ever. While the handsome design was heavily inspired by the 1970 original, the L322 was a thoroughly modern car, with monocoque construction, a class-leading cabin and immense luxury.

**2005-13**
RANGE ROVER SPORT

Three-door Range Stormer concept from 2004 morphed into this radical five-door production version.

**2007-**
FREELANDER 2

Hatchback tailgate replaced side-hinged boot door - indicative of a more grown-up, family-oriented vehicle.

**2011-**
RANGE ROVER EVOQUE

Evoque is to the Freelander what Sport is to the Range Rover; a more road-biased, sportier car.

**2012-**
RANGE ROVER L405

Clever use of aluminium cuts 400kg from weight.

**2013-**
RANGE ROVER SPORT L494

All-new, all aluminium Sport promises to be the best drive in the Land Rover stable, with its sophisticated suspension setup and improved off-road ability.

| 1998 | 1999 | 2000 | 2001 | 2002 | 2003 | 2004 | 2005 | 2006 | 2007 | 2008 | 2009 | 2010 | 2011 | 2012 | 2013 | 2014 |

**AND FINALLY...**
**RANGE ROVER SPORT 2013**
It seems fitting to end with Land Rover's latest,
the new Sport. Here's to another 65 years of
an iconic British company and the cars it builds